A Tapestry OF Thoughts

Edited by
Allison Jones

First published in Great Britain in 2010 by:
Forward Press
Remus House
Coltsfoot Drive
Peterborough
PE2 9JX
Telephone: 01733 890099
Website: www.forwardpress.co.uk

Foreword

Here at Forward Press our aim has always been to provide a bridge to publication for unknown poets and allow their work to reach a wider audience. We believe that poetry should not be exclusive or elitist but available to be accessed and appreciated by all.

We hope you will agree that our latest collection with its combination of traditional and modern verse is one that everyone can enjoy. Whether you prefer humourous rhymes or poignant odes there is something inside these pages that will suit every reader's taste.

We are very proud to present this anthology and we are sure it will provide entertainment and inspiration for years to come.

Contents

The Poems

Life's Simple Pleasures

Simple Pleasures Are Priceless

Old age has become my category, with the disability label thrown in.
Did I think my life over? To have that thought is a sin.
I don't mind that there is no more dancing, nor propping myself up by a bar.
A cup of tea has become my indulgence and I can no longer travel too far.
I love to wander in my garden, stopping to pull a weed.
As I progress I pull many more and can almost do it with ease.
Can't wait to plant out new blossoms, I'm slow, but I can still do.
'Tis more fun in my own backyard now my gallivanting days are through.
In mid-summer I shall take my chair and sit quietly in my plot.
Look around and am contented realising what a lot I've got.
Only housework is a real chore for me though it shouldn't bother me so.
I'm not expecting the Queen to visit me so I can allow a little dust to show.

Why not!

Rosie Hues

What Is Bliss?

Having time to stand and stare,
While looking at nothing at all,
Not having to always check the clock,
Or worrying about rushing off to work,

Just listening to the silence of the world,
Hearing the whispering of the earth,
Telling that you about its second birth,

The smell of newly baked bread,
The sponge cake that has risen in the oven,
Scones fresh and warm with jam and cream,
With that all important cup of tea,
Putting your feet up in front of the open fire,
Settling down with a good book to read,
Being nice and warm when it's cold outside

Pauline Uprichard

My Beloved Child

My sweet beloved child,
for this is truly what you are
to see your eyes shine back at me
is like looking at the stars!

You have captivated my heart and soul,
you who give me such joy and pleasure
the greatest things of love and peace
for you alone are my treasure.

It's the way that you smile, so carefree,
I know your heart is filled with love
for as I look unto the heavens
I thank the very God of love.

Yes you have such amazing energy,
as you run and dance around the place
and yet you are such a caring little boy
so very funny and yet filled with grace!

I just want to pick you up and cuddle you,
to say I love you a thousand times
and to hear you whisper I love you
for this day my child you are mine!

Simon Foderingham

Sewing With Love

I have a great passion for many things,
Sewing my first and last love.
Have always enjoyed making things,
Designing, sometimes, for embroidery,
Of cushion covers, with beads.
Concentration is the word,
Where and ever it needs.
Fabrics a joy to handle,
As the garment shape, takes place,
Hard to say, how the magic begins,
As the person in mind, who you care for,
Tries it on and says,
'I feel like a million dollars in this,'
'Give us a kiss.'
Then, of course, when it's become a favourite thing,
Worn nearly every day, gets a bit threadbare,
Won't throw it away.
I made my late partner a waistcoat,
A favourite garment he wore,
Still in his wardrobe today,
Cannot bear to throw it away,
So it's me, back to poetry, for another day.

Mabel Deb Moore

It's Interesting (My Garden)

What's cuter than to garden
To kick out the weeds
To eke out flower beds
Though some may feel beat
The chat is crisp over
The light garden fence
The neighbours spin stories
Not any song and dance
Sleep comes quietly at night
The garden work takes me there
My crying limbs see if it's right -
The softness of my bed
Not at all times but
Often I pluck a nightmare
About my garden
Being destroyed uncared

Muhammad Khurram Salim

Boats On The Thames At Henley

Shadowy hulks amass
with subtle 'sas' . . .

Sweet scent of oil,
and sun reflecting on the brass

Whispering willows weep
over sleek hulks of boats
Mirrored
as they slice the silvery silence . . .

Scenes from which dreams are made

Edna Sparkes

A Two-Bit Day

A two-bit day walking in the rain
Quiet and lonesome in the city
Don't give yourself away today
You ain't lucky, you ain't pretty

I was raised in a crazy place
They shook my hand, slapped my face
Some were enemies, some were mates
Some were quiet, some were crazed

Some have gone and went
Abandoned love, left this life
All for the lousy dealership
Of drugs, guns and knives

Some of the rest have kids
Houses, prowl-cars and wives
Pay all their bills on time
Tow the drunken party line

Some left, some couldn't leave
The chain was too strong
They were born to believe
In good times to come along

I wish I were made of summer
But it's winter in my veins
I'd crop the bolts of time too
I'd ride the prairie if I had to

Everybody, every day said the same thing
Which changed absolutely nothing

Feelings there are no words for
Stall in the heart and never fall

John Harkin

Lost In Dreams

Daydreaming is what I like doing best
I am in my own little world obsessed
Forming beautiful pictures in my mind
The people I meet are of various kinds
I fly to exotic places and foreign lands
And visit places, oh so big and so grand
When feeling low, I switch on my dreams
Enjoying myself what I might have been
Losing myself in my make-believe land
Going to the moon and many places unplanned
Shut myself off from this stressful life
Avoiding this world of trouble and strife
I often join in where playboys lurk
Then it's down to earth and back to work.

Leonard A G Butler

Mercies

We've earned a little money,
so we sit in some sad café
to talk about silly things,

where there is solace in tea,
in stirring it around,
in watching it settle,

coming slowly to a stop.
There is comfort,
in the roundness of the cups,

in the way the pot sits,
fat, like a porcelain pig,
making my nose look big

when I stare up close.
And when we finish one cup,
we know there are two more

safe in the pot,
like a little money in the bank,
for which - this small mercy -

we give thanks.

Francis Barker

Intoxication

Bitter mingles with sweet; suffocation
A perfect square, deep brown temptation
A blend of magic, a touch of intoxication

An aquarelle sky, an artist's interpretation
Rich vibrant ribbons of inspiration
A blend of magic, a touch of intoxication

Crystalline notes, beautiful vibration
Floating in air dripping with anticipation
A blend of magic, a touch of intoxication

The smell of rain, soft purification
Giving the world much needed hydration
A blend of magic, a touch of intoxication

Soft fingers of air caress with love's infatuation
Shaping a face, molding hair, sculpting elation
A blend of magic, a touch of intoxication

A cocktail of memories, feelings, sensation
Mixed with a shot of unstoppable exhilaration
A touch of magic, a blend of intoxication.

Lucie McMurtry

Rainbow

A colourful piece of fabric on the sky
It comes just after the gloomy rain.
When the Golden Sun starts to shine!
I want to touch it. Give me a pair of wings to fly!
What a pleasure it is to watch a rainbow
I wish I could capture it somehow
It is too long to measure
And an unforgettable pleasure!

Piyush Sriram

Dawn Chorus

A solitary blackbird heralds a new day,
Another answer echoes not too far away.
Their dialogue continues for several minutes till
A lark joins the chorus, with a call that's loud and shrill.
Then the chatter of a robin, unmistakably distinct
And the 'caw-caw' of a crow, harsh-sounding and succinct.
A brace of collared doves are the next to contribute,
With their billing and their cooing; determined, resolute.
By this time, all the other birds have added to the throng
And the company of voices are united in one song.
There's something reassuring and soothing, I must say,
About these choristers at the dawning of the day.

Heather Pickering

Life's Simple Pleasures

The smell of freshly mown grass,
The ticking of the clock,
The hooting of an owl,
The slowness of a snail,
The taste of your favourite meal
Will always do the trick,
A bunch of fresh flowers
Will always smell divine,
The smell, when you open a book
At its very first page.
All of these are simple pleasures,
The simple pleasures of life.

Amber Kelsey

Bumblies, Crumblies And Fumblies

Don't bother a Bumblie
and it won't bother you!
You do watch any Bumblie with some dread
as it may bump into you where you tread.
It is a great friend of the bumblebee
that whirrs its wings by a flower you may see.
Each delights in ultra-violet rays
which enhance their lifestyles on summer days.
Don't bother the Bumblie
because all this is true.

How careless the Crumblie!
More so than you or me.
Its roofless castle losing stone on stone
nor does that ruin crumble all alone.
Cottages around crumble just to match.
If you entered one, no doubt you would catch
people eating cake with crumbs on faces
Of that sponge cake they would leave no traces.
Though careless all Crumblies
few of their crumbs you'll see.

Forgive foolish Fumblies
even though they're not dumb . . .
The china that you cherished all broken
Your last crystal wineglass too - a token.
Of the damage any Fumblie can do.
The fridge - and the TV - not working too?
Do not hand them anything marked *fragile*.
Bound to be found shattered after a while . . .
Forgive foolish Fumblies -
all fingers and no thumb!

Chris Creedon

A Walk In The Park

Whilst walking in the local park, during the month of May
I heard a cuckoo calling informing all that summer is nigh
The trees holding their parasols of green towards the overhead sun
Nearby bushes covered in pink or white blooms
In the shade late spring flowers dancing in the slight breeze
Along the twisting footpaths I stroll towards the lake
The ducks and swans tend their young, teaching them to swim and feed
Children in their boats with oars akimbo
Parents shouting for them to be careful
Side-stepping the steep embankment down to the river
Sauntering, watching the eddies and flows as the rushing water travels downstream
Sitting dreaming of where it may have been, in the mountains or moorlands
Ascending towards the bridle path, I meet two horses with riders aloft
Making their way to the field where they canter and trot
Jumping the man-made fences to their hearts' content
Returning to the main walkway, passing the children's playground and golf course
Towards the highway as home I must return

Margaret Monaghan

Reservoir

From a bridge of sighs I look to where
This man-made flooded valley lies.
An eerie place.
Shrouded now in swirling mists,
The spirits of the past perhaps
From once a gentle landscape,
Fertile, grazed and tilled,
Filled with sights of mortal toil,
A cottage by a church in fields of standing wheat.
A mill and snake-like leat.

On callous depths, a guilty mirror face beguiles
With sweeping curve of siren smiles
Ill at ease, dark and brooding.
Hidden by armies, of glowering trees,
Sullen at this barrier to progress.
Nestling restless in their whispering embrace.

Caressed by barely stirring down breeze
Glittering wavelets march in unison
Towards the leeward quarter,
Passing beneath the bobbing Mallard, unconcerned.
Towards far banks and muddy shallows,
With gentle slap-slap of lapping water.

In startling all-white plumage, overhead an egret flaps
Across a window to an agitated sky,
Searching for a place to feed
Along the fringes of the rustling reed.

An angler casts his line and somewhere out of sight
Emerging from the night, sounds of life.
So far and yet so near.

A sense of peace is somehow absent here.
Too many spirits haunt this place, this paradise for fools.
For here, amongst the mud and debris of a town
The wretched come to drown - lost souls

And here for them, the searchers come to seek and find
Death - in beauty of a kind.

Ben Corde

Life's Simple Pleasures

Slowly setting sunsets
Indigo lakes
Massive snow-capped mountains
Plopping raindrops
Loving hugs
Everlasting friendship

Perfectly coloured dragonflies
Lovingly tended flowers
Elegant butterflies
Aquamarine oceans
Softly bubbling streams
Under-the-sea coral reefs
Rocky cliffs
Energising fresh air
Star-studded nights

Lily Westcott

Simple Pleasures

A bunch of fiery-red tulips
In beautiful summer

A cute snow leopard purring silently
But loud enough for people to hear.

A gentle breeze on a glamorous countryside
Lovely, pleasant fresh air.

A glorious sunset over a reflecting sea
As the tide goes out again.

A fantastic dinner, delicious pasta
The best food in the world.

A head on a pillow, snoring peacefully
At the end of a perfect day . . .

Owen Thurston

When Caroline Came Round To Tea

Such poshness as you never ever have seen,
Not even if you were a king or a queen,
Or the richest of sultans as ever there's been,
At least it looked that way to me:
The table-wine flowed just like water that day,
It took three blokes to cart all the empties away,
Buck House garden parties were never so gay,
As when Caroline came round to tea.

Mum got dolled up in her flash Sunday best,
And spent about two an' 'alf hours getting dressed,
And then said, 'Come in, dear, excuse all the mess,
I haven't been in long, you see.'
But she'd spent all day cleaning the house, front to back,
And she'd dusted and polished-up every knick-knack,
And on one occasion, she'd hoovered the cat
For when Caroline came round to tea.

The table was class, really fit for a toff,
With Granny's hand-crocheted pre-war table cloff,
And the bread with the polythene bag taken off,
Cut in triangles, like on TV,
And the butter was unwrapped and put in a dish,
And the milk in a jug, (not the bottle!) how swish!
And we had some cheese pie, only Mum called it quiche,
When Caroline came round to tea.

We had two separate knives for our butter and jam,
And another one still, for our pickles and ham,
And Mum got out another to cut the fruit flan,
'Stead of wiping one on her pinny,
And we all had a spoon each for stirring our char,
And tongs for the sugar! I felt like a star!
You've never seen anything so lah-de-dah,
As when Caroline came round to tea.

It seemed such a shame everything should go wrong,
Especially after Mum laboured so long,
But the wine bottle cork flew aloft, and went 'dong'!
Then it fell in Dad's trifle, you see,
He looked so surprised when his trifle went splat!
It flew out of his dish, and it dropped in his lap,
Then his hand knocked his teacup, which fell on the cat,
And then Caroline giggled with glee!

The cat, jerked awake by this pain in its head,
Leapt up on the table, amidst all the bread,
And I couldn't repeat all the things that Mum said
To our salad-draped, buttered moggie!
But though Caroline's visit turned into a fray,
She can come back again, around Christmas, I'd say,
Cos Mum said, 'It won't half be a bloody cold day
Before Caroline comes back to tea!'

Mick Nash

My Favourite Things

I like to see my mum when I come home from school
I like to hear music when we do Wake and Shake
I like to feel the touch of wood
I like to touch my mummy when I cuddle her
I like to smell flowers in my garden
I like to taste melon dribbling on my chin
I like it when I've been really good and I get a treat
These are a few of my favourite things.

Victoria Slann

My Favourite Things

I like to see my mum when I come home from school
I like to hear my cats purr when I stroke them
I like to feel happy
I like to touch my boy cat's fur, it is soft
I like to smell chips cooking for my tea
I like to taste cakes and chocolate, I like mint flavour
I like it when my cat comes when I tap on my sofa
These are a few of my favourite things.

Aaron Crosby Jewell

Timetable

Time is a factor
You can't ignore
Rushing hither and thither
Time waits for no man
As the saying goes
Have I time for this?
Have I time for that?
Time the vital issue
No going back
Only in recollections
Joy - happiness - sadness
All weave the pattern of life
Time being
The name of the game
The game of life
Like the old grandfather clock
We plod on regardless
Time and time again
Waiting for Old Father Time
To see if the
New Year
Will be our 'dream year'
If not: dream on.

Margaret Parnell

Life Drops

It rained today on the windowpane
Pitter-patter the sound,
Soothing the angry storm
Soothing the room.
Pitter-patter on the rooftop,
The walls that cried.
A peaceful sound the rain that fell
Like a big waterfall falling from the heavens
And life begins wherever it lands
Making new pathways
In a desert land.

R Sunshine

The Gift Of Noise!

I love the sound of burning sticks and flowing pentatonic licks.
And place names such as John O'Groats, or merging acappella notes.
Though there's many from the Manx TT, nothing beats the beautiful MV!
Or possibly the Honda Six, prepared by grand prix mechanics
Seldom heard now Rolls Royce Merlin, the Lancaster with all four whirlin'

The natural world inspires awe, like crashing waves mapping the shore.
From rattling Jackdaws in winter trees, to laid back July Bumblebees.
The deafening march of lava flow, tectonic shift from deep below
Or weird enigmatic Whale song, harking from where men don't belong
Silence-inducing waterfalls, nocturnal drawn-out canine calls.

Complex, simplistic, twelve bar blues, with missing notes in ones and twos.
Your child's first signature laughter, language growing daily after.
The yearly dip into Christmas hits, Mr Jimmy's ground-breaking lead bits.
Starling announcing spring is here, the Cuckoo bidding summer near.
Ruthless alarm, blaring away, then silence, because it's Sunday!

Geoff Birchall

Clean As A Whistle!

A new blade to my razor
Like a newly-honed scythe to the hay!
I repent of all the mornings spent irksomely slaving away
With a weapon that wouldn't cut butter hot!
Just to feel that sheer cleanness of the ocean wave
As though a biting wind just swept across the tundra.
I won't be bothering with aftershave!

The girls will exult after months of 'roughware'
To close with the smoothness of a babe's derrière.

Tony Sainsbury

To The Naughty Chair She Went

O Erica Jane,
Who slapped Grandma across the face,
Who slurped her water bottle all over the place,
To the naughty chair she went,
Who ran away laughing,
Thinking she was in a race,

While scribbling her felt-tip pen over the settee,
O pretty Madame went, laughing merrily,
A cute bundle of trouble,
Being naughty behind Mum and Dad,
But Grandad clocked her cute little face,

O so innocent with chocolate over all the table-lace,
To the naughty chair she went,
Crying and screaming,
'O it wasn't me, Mummy,
Grandad did it, not I.'

For her escapade did not end there,
As she scratched marks all over the telly,
As she sat in her naughty chair,
Grinning from ear to ear,
Whilst pulling out all the stuffing of her teddy bear,

While escaping a good telling off,
From Mum and Dad,
O Erica Jane,
In the supermarket she ran away,
Eating sweets and chocolate,

As all the staff praised her,
O what a cute little child,
With her hair like Goldilocks,
And a bright smile of an angel,
O so bright and gay,

As all the cans came crashing down,
While all the shoppers gathered round,
Little Miss Erica Jane gave a frown,
'Oh, it was Grandad, not I.'
As an old granny gave her a silver crown.

James S Cameron

Feeding The Ducks

He stood alone by the lake,
an old man, in a coat
that had seen better days ten years ago.
Carefully crumbling bread
that might have done him some good,
he threw it to the cacophony
of ducks squabbling in the water.
'Come on my beauties,' he said
'no pushing and shoving, now.'
Gently he threw some to the shy ones
pattering on the edge of the mob.
Then turning away he called an old black dog
with a grey muzzle and arthritic legs.
'That's it for today,' he said
'all the excitement's done now.'
And together they walked slowly
towards the gate.

Gillian Peall

Fragrance Of Roses

The smell of roses
Drifts intermittently
On the breeze

Desperately trying
To perfume the
Polluted world
We live in

The fragrance
Hitchhikes on
The back of
Diesel and petrol fumes

And the occasional
Waft of cigarette smoke
Roses sweetening our senses
But not overpowering them

Gaelynne Pound

The Chocolate Box

A box of tricks, sticky fingertips
As chocolate sauce licks strawberry lips.
A chocolate box of hidden delights
The caramel rocks with sweet surprise.
A jewellery box with diamond truffles
And vanilla ice cream clouds the puzzle.
A jack-in-the-box with juicy prizes
Lures us into confectionery crisis.
The chocolate shop has everything
From pick and mix to Champagne Pink.
A selection box of the sweetest dreams
A feast that never lets you sleep.

Craig Shuttleworth

It's A Wonderful Piece Of Art

Not now later please
Cut your cloth
According to the tailor

Soon! Soon!
Whenever you run
Turn around look back

Walking all along the street
Neat bit of work
Got to dash find some cash

Coming home
From town
To the flat

Justice will out
Truth to tell - the poem!
It's a Wonderful Piece of Art

What might it mean?
I dare to say
My poem gains praise

So should I speak
Of what life is to art!
Appreciation: dedication: A Wonderful Piece of Art!

Stella Thompson

The 'Jurassic' Coast

A silver ocean just like glass,
Where crystal waters lie;
With rocks so like a Grecian vase,
Its land and sea and sky,
In fading light - the setting sun,
So tints the distant cloud,
The stars at night when day is done,
With dolphins in the sound;
It's here along this ancient coast,
Uncovered by the sea,
So many creatures long time lost,
Revealed that once roamed free;
So many fossils land and shore,
A world no longer here,
All brought to light at the ocean's door,
Appearing year to year;
And as the sun at night descends
From Lyme round to The Bill,
The rocks and cliffs from end to end,
A seascape never still;
The shore, the world - no other bay,
Can match where you might be,
A place where God so has his say,
Its land and rocks and sea . . .

Tom Ritchie

A Quiet Morning Sat In The Cemetery

A quiet morning sat in the cemetery
Amidst a veil of consecrated mist
A contentment and calmness and feeling of serenity
A land of eternal bliss

An overwhelming absence of zest and agility
A king-sized bed of six feet deep
A quiescence and ease and profound tranquillity
A place of eternal sleep

A raven perched on a bough of a gnarled old oak
Stone headboards with dreamers lay under
The stillness and silence of the epitaph folk
Engaged in eternal slumber

The soft white doves in the larch and beech
Sweet blossoms in bloom on the cherry tree
A motionless world of relaxation and peace
. . . A quiet morning sat in the cemetery.

Peter T Ridgway

The Garden

As we sit within the garden
Listening to its magic sounds
Watching the butterflies flutter,
From flower to flower as in magic dance

The bees drone endlessly around
Gossamer webs of silver strands
As spiders, lay in their traps
Waiting for the strand to sing

Poems dreams into a magic time
Of many gift and prayers
There for all to see and travel
When they read the first page

R Mills

A Smile

A lot is in a smile - it's phrase that's not been said,
A smile does warm you up inside - it goes straight to your head.
It's a simple way of saying, 'Hi!' or 'How are you today?'
It makes you glad just for a second. It's a feeling you wish would stay.
A smile takes away your troubles and fills you up with hope,
It is the highlight of the day: the perfect horoscope.
But a smile isn't formed just with your mouth; half the magic is from your eyes,
Smiles from the world have accompanied so many 'Hellos' and 'Goodbyes'!
When you're smiled at you are sailing over stars on a silver moon,
A smile is never ever late and you can't get one too soon -
They make your life worth living, a smile you'll never forget,
Smiles lift your mood when you are glum and stop you feeling so upset.

Maria Dixon

Life

So many desires and aspirations to fulfil!
Man: Life is too short!
Life: You've still got time

Lazing about now; I don't care!
Man: Life is too long!
Life: Time's running out!

Hey, who switched off the lights!
Man: Life, where have you gone?
Life: I've run out.

Sonia Kauser

The Colour Of Rain

I can see the world through your reflection.
Your watery hands kissing the dust of my homeland.
I can hear the drumming of heartbeats
Through the door that you open.
I can feel the clothes you are wearing
The woes you are sharing
The dreams you are caring
Through the colour of rain.

Natalie Williams

Turning Away

We knew it would happen,
We've arrived at this day.
Your life is now changing,
And you're turning away.

You're starting a new life,
I'll return to the old.
For the dye has been cast,
And the stories been told.

As the snow starts to melt,
And spring pushes on.
When the buds start to bloom,
I know you'll be gone.

Living under the same sun,
But in worlds far apart.
Remember I loved you,
And gave you my heart.

Look back on the good times,
Like a bright sunny day.
No regrets and no tears,
Just you turning away.

Allan Wood

'Oliver' Extravaganza

Enter the doors of the Drury Lane theatre in London
designed by architect Sir Christopher Wren
founder Thomas Killrew - influenced by Palais de
Tuleries in Paris designed by Gaspare Vigarani
large foyer and statue of Shakespeare lead by John
Cheere. Hangs handsome 'patent' board holders
since 1663. Mahogany war memorial names in gold -
members of theatrical profession who fell in
Great War. In stalls and circle rotunda statues and
busts of Garrick, Keen, Novello, Dan Leno

Forbes-Robertson, Doric columns, painting of Keen as
Brutus. Climb Princes and Kings staircases,
impressive rotunda, magnificent green grand salon,
sweeping staircases, breathtaking chandeliers
enjoy Lionel Bart's musical masterpiece, 'Oliver'
Dickens' novel written 1837, poor houses,
child exploitation - criminality, desperation, four
cholera outbreaks. Unique 80ft deep stage
technology was naval based on blocks of pulleys used on
sailing ships. Boys sing, 'Food, glorious food'

Oliver asks Beadle - 'Please Sir, I want some more.'
Fluidity and rhythm, episodic story,
quick varied moves, wit, style, 'One Boy For Sale' -
'That's Your Funeral' - 'Where Is Love?'
'It's Clear We're Going To Get Along' - 'Consider Yourself Our
Mate' - 'I'll Do Anything' - 'Pick A Pocket Or Two' - 'Be Back
Soon' - 'Oom Pah Pah' - 'As Long As He Needs Me'
'Who Will Buy My Sweet Red Roses' - 'Muffins For Tea' flower sellers, matchgirls.

Nell Gwynn stage debut age 15 in John Dryden's 'The Indian Queen' 1665
David Garrick died 20 January 1779 and interred Westminster Abbey close to
Shakespeare's monument - 2,283 seating three-tiered, below boxes at sides
experience aura, craft, music, actors, choreography - wander in Covent Garden
dine in cafés - breathtaking memories of a perfect day.

Patricia Turpin

The Road Of Life

When the road ahead is weary, light is growing dark or dim
The path before you seems scary, shaky, insecure or grim
Pace yourself, don't rush ahead, take one step at a time
There's no mountain, hill or peak that you cannot climb
There's naught to fear in the journey, roads alone to take
That path you tread each day, is a one you alone can make?
Remember, there's always an end somewhere on each road
A place to rest your weary head, unburdening any old load
As the darkness ever gives way to a brand new light of day
Keep this in your heart to reassure you along on your way
The path we make is a solitary one, sadly we can't go back
It's a one way road we make with each step taken in its track
Returning is done by memory alone, some places we avoid
Others we often look back upon, relishing tearfully overjoyed
Steps into here are but alone in memory, places to often assure
Some are sad and tearful, there are many we chose to detour
No one knows the path of life, no one has a map of the way
Its very route we make ourselves, with every passing day
It started in brilliance and light, signs of a new creation
Guides to keep you right, steering wisely with consideration
The day came when you walked this path, trod its road alone
Every passing night and morn, you're ever heading back home
It will end in a dark, brief moment, turning yet again to light
The ending now, two roads to choose, only one of those is right?
At this point, no man can help point you left or right, they say
This all depends on those footprints you've taken day by day?

Christopher Slater

A Smile Is Never Far Away

A message, a letter, a card,
Or a call breaks a smile
A good deed, a thank you, a little praise
That makes the day worthwhile

The Friday night feeling
That comes in the closing part of the afternoon
All the promises of a weekend
That will be here very soon

Hallowe'en, Fireworks of the oncoming autumn
Knowing Christmas is not far around bend
The Childlike nostalgia fills the ether that
Softens the sadness of the summer's end

A happy ending at the turn of the page
At the end of the week, a well-deserved wage
The ring school bell of half-past three
Where I always found my
Grandad as always, waiting for me

Stephen Prout

Painted In The Past

It gathered dust, 'The Painted Lass'
A Masterpiece of a good artist,
He took the risk, and explore the mist,
Into the valley and home,
Of the painted lass.

The lass, you see, is of noble birth,
Came to love a noble art,
Arts that makes the artist smart,
Fortune and Glory, there he start,
She undressed herself, and smile with art.

Years gone by, the artist see,
To his fortune and glory wished by she,
Abandoned by noble kin, because of he,
Sold millions of, 'The Painted Lass',
Though art should has?

The artist went worldwide,
Bring more fortune and tried,
Love of luxury, and be wild,
And forgot, to be wise,
That his fortune, no more in rise.

More years gone by, he's in poverty,
No one adores his artistry,
Not bold enough, to take the liberty,
And give up his misery,
Though art should he?

The lass . . . he thought at last,
Thought again . . . no more a lass,
Try to find her whereabouts,
And bring the time, when he's about,
To say his thanks when they fall apart.

He saw the lass, no more a lass
The 'Painted Lass', no more to see,
So cruel to be, Time tends to be
His arts no more,
So as he.

Angelita Redfern

My Sunday View

Looking out my window,
On a Sunday afternoon,
Looking out across the houses.
Thinking of a tune,
Everywhere calm, watching seagulls fly,

Families indoors resting after Sunday roast,
Wrapping up warm for a stroll by the coast.
Roofs, flat or pointed, there are so many,
With chimney pots gently puffing smoke,
Are they burning wood or are they burning coke?

Robins, blue tits and chaffinches come visiting for food,
Just throw them the bread where you are stood.
A rusty old swing stands in the garden alone!
Does it creak or does it moan?
An old broken down church in need of repair
Do the people really care?

This wraps up my view from my cosy armchair.

Jo Chapman

Take Your Time, Don't Rush!

Take your time, don't rush,
Think logical,
No need to fly,
Let the winds carry you,
To far-off places,
Full of warm air and smiles,
Take your time,
Enjoy life for a while,
Relish in its splendour,
Isn't it amazing to be alive?
Look around, take your time.

Sit by a lake and watch the ripples,
Take a walk through long grass,
And let your legs be tickled,
Hold your partner in your arms,
Tight and safe,
Give the right feeling,
That you will never walk away,
That you'll be there no matter what,
Loving them with passion,
Taking in their every feature,
Adoring before you, what your eyes see.
Cuddle your daughter or son,
Let them know they have a mum or dad,
That loves them, respects them,
Tell them that they make you proud,
Love and cherish them,
Watch them grow up,
They make mistakes,
Run back to your safe arms,
And you make them better,
Then send them off again,
Into the world to live,
Find a job, partner and be happy.
Ring your friends up out the blue,
Invite them all round,
Switch on the music,

Crack open a bottle,
And have a party,
Joke and be naughty,
Like you're ten again,
Wake up with a hangover,
But smile 'cause of all the fun you had,
It was worth the pain,
Throbbing in your foggy head,
Just another hour, stay snuggled up in bed.
Take a holiday,
Sit by the sea and have a picnic,
Taking in the salty breeze,
Watching the kids chasing around,
With the gulls soaring above,
Waves lapping against the shore,
Blue skies and golden sands,
Sun baking you brown,
Sandwiches and ice cream,
Cold fizzy beer to wash it down,
Sand stretching for miles,
More than your eyes can see,
Are you happy at this place?
Like a flower to a bee.
Or book a table in a restaurant,
With a person that you adore,
All dressed up and smelling nice,
Gazing across to them so near,
Wanting to lushly whisper,
Sweet nothings in their ear,
Taking in their every move,
They make your heart beat fast,
So quick and clear,
Wanting to save every moment,
Making the night with them last.
They are your one and only,
Waiter more champagne in the glass!
There are a million things to make us happy,
We just have to look and see,
The magic that is all around us,
You just have to believe,
So take your time,

Don't rush this thing called life,
Savour it; wrap it in your heart,
Safe and protected,
Free from the scratches,
Of life's harsh claws,
Love it, live it,
Grab all things tight,
For life is worth living,
A magical, mystery life's delight.

Emma McNamara

Breakfast

A symphony in progress amidst
Murmur from swarming tables . . .

At the counter,
An expectant crowd awaits their orders.
The chaos beyond the counter is the kitchen:
A delightful lesson in supply chain.
Ten people co-ordinate the chaos,
Water boils, appliances hiss,
Tea and coffee steam,
Vegetables are being sliced,
Spices are being ground,
The floor is being scrubbed,
Utensils are being washed,
Flames rise higher
As one of the chefs deftly
Maneuvers a sizzling oversized pan,
Nobody waits long;
Orders are fulfilled promptly,
And plates displaying varied fare
Appear at the counter.
I had once read that
The kitchen is a true meritocracy.
Well, this one is an orchestra too.

In this stand-in eatery,
I, a satisfied patron, part audience
Have enjoyed a gratifying
Sunday breakfast.

Aditya Nabial

Keep On Smiling

A smiling face makes all the difference
When you are feeling low
It fills you with fresh hope
And helps your heart to glow

A smiling face to greet you
A chance for you to speak
Makes the day worthwhile
Gives comfort through the week

A smiling face makes people happy
In life's drama it does uplift
So keep on smiling, it is God's work
And a very precious gift

Catherine Armstrong

Baby Poet

My Grandsons have grown, quite a bit
Lewis, the eldest, can 'make' his words fit
Like me he is a bit of a poet
He takes the time to make a rhyme and show it.

'It's going to be a long, long time, Nan'
As the words he tries to find.
Try as he may, many boyish distractions on his mind.
They take him back on a train in time
Yes, Lewis, 'It's going to be a long, long time'

His brain clicks on 'Clickety-clack'
Just like the train along the track.
Determined as ever, he 'beavers on'
His verses short, medium and long.

'What's the time, Lewis?' He turns and smiles
'Nanna, it's going to take a long, long time.'

Ellen Spiring

Mood Lifted

I was feeling rather low on Sunday morning,
Then I heard repetitive peal of phone ringing.
'Hello, Gran,' small voice said, 'Got on my dress - it's red,'
'Hi, sweetheart,' I replied, 'I've just got out of bed.'

'Can I come over, Gran and visit you today?'
'Oh, that would be great darling, I've a new game we can play.'
Immediately my gloomy mood lightened,
Hastily I dressed and my black shoelaces tightened.

Decided granddaughter and I'd walk to the shop,
Well, I would stroll, however, all the way she would hop.
Buy a magazine we could both read and enjoy,
They sometimes contain stickers and a plastic toy.

A tap on the front door signalled my angel had arrived,
Not sure without her that weekend I'd have survived.
Two hours passed before she helped me scrape some carrots,
From the garden we had lifted a bunch of shallots.

After a healthy meal, we watched a video,
Madam had a long bubble bath and she had to go.
'Thank you, darling,' I said to her, 'today has been fun,'
She replied, 'Yes, Gran, let's soon share another one.'

Susan Mullinger

Apart, Sisters Together Hoping

It was cheeky, plucky
On my sixtieth birthday
To ask you for a memory
In frame and a card.
You are loved.
No blaming for the brushes
With which we were tarred.

You militarily-managed the party.
In good supply-chatter, wine, fare.
A wand-wave of stardust
May have helped at Cerveteri
To touch us in that little Square.

Our gathering was in the evening.
Boys running on the grass, hot.
I blew out the candles with gusto.
I relished the attention I got.

The separate souls we came from
Kept things on their chest.
Not there for each other - no example Godly.
With appearances were impressed.
We will build on this backdrop
For the young ones,
A more open, positive best.

Italy partially claimed you.
The land of style, cornetti, song.
Bonds to be cemented
When your sixtieth celebration looms
And now Bud, it won't be long.

Carol Sherwood

Butterfly Of Harmony

Butterfly of harmony,
You flutter in summer your destiny,
You're like a dainty fairy queen,
Fluttering in the summer scene,
You love to flutter as high as a kite,
You love to flutter in the shadows of light,
You really love being a high flyer,
The gentle breeze guides you wherever you desire,
Gardens, meadows, woodlands too,
Where the bluebells are like a sea of blue,
You love the breathtaking views,
The colours reds, pinks, yellows and blues,
You rest on a flower as the warm sun beats down,
You're like a jewel in a crown.

Joanna Maria John

Oddities

Mollie took Gary for a walk
He was very slow
She asked her mum if they could walk in the street
Mother quickly answered no
With a hair toggle for a harness
And a ribbon for a lead
They walked right round the garden
It took a very long time indeed
Because Gary is a slow coach
An African snail she loves to bits
To see Mollie taking him for a stroll
Leaves the whole of the family in fits.

Daphne Fryer

Moment In Sainsbury's

After work, shopping,
Oh, I can't be bothered in my head,
Only there's no food in the fridge,
Or cupboard,
So I gotta go.

Sainsbury's,
The fruit and veg aisles,
How about bananas,
Too many in a packet,
Never sure about the green ones,
Woman in the way,
Just grab those,
Grab them.

OK, bit of salad,
No cucumbers,
No cucumbers,
I can't believe there are no cucumbers
No cucumbers,
OK, there are no cucumbers.

How about bread,
The bread aisle,
'Yeah, but if we invite him to the house, then we'll have to invite Carl . . .'
Who said that?
Looking up,
Face frozen in difficult decision making,
Muffins or crumpets?
Two well-to-do teenagers,
Walking towards me,
One talking
The other staring,
Staring and staring,
His friend has stopped to see who he's staring at,
I'm wondering who he's staring at,
He's staring at me.

Why is he staring at me?
Oh, God, what have I got on my face,
My gargoyle muffins or crumpet face.

Then a thought at the back of my head,
Did he fancy me?
Perhaps he fancied me,
Naw, don't be silly, I'm old enough to be his mum
I've got a boyfriend.

But that was the moment,
Daydreaming about being a Mrs Robinson,
I could be a Mrs Robinson and come to his party instead of Carl
And then I burp,
An acidic burp,
Rennie, mustn't forget the Rennie
And the moment is gone.

Haidée Chutur

Morning Constitutional

Morning constitutional walk
For the benefit of one's health,
Nice to stop to talk
To old friends Bill and Elf.

One of life's simple pleasures,
The folk one meets
Whilst taking life at leisure,
Walking constitutional beat.

Stop to have a chat with Dane and Shally,
They've been together for years,
Never married,
They were known as Good Years.

Good morning or good day,
The cheery greeting folk say.

Bryan Clarke

Gwen's Trinket Box

Gwen sat before her vanity mirror
Jewellery box brimming with trinkets to treasure,
Father's gold watch, an engagement ring
Sparkling gems which gave her great pleasure,
In a small leather box - a pair of pearl earrings
A gift when she came of age,
Three of Gran's diamond hair slides
In the twenties these were all the rage,
A butterfly brooch in finest gold
Belonged to Mother when she was a girl,
And a dainty fan with silver tassels
Heavily decorated with mother-of-pearl,
A bracelet from the twins and a locket from John
Romantic memories of a happy life,
Childhood days, teenage years
And now as a Mother and Wife.

Jean Mackenzie

Steel Growing

From the seeds that are sown
Our little trees have grown.
This little tree
Waves its branches when full of glee.
Those roots I knew would hold,
Though frost and icy winds blew too cold.
Now these begin to melt,
When sun and warmth are felt.
Once again we'll see those blossoms made of metal
That show the prettiest, the daintiest of petals.

Clare Todd

Landscape As Muse (The Ancient Ones)

Estranged, three ancient ones
Silent on the brow of the hill - fixed in tortured shapes as the wind moulded them
Their fragrance in blossom assures again berries
Ancient hawthorns are again as brides in splendour
Coy girls as a breeze flounces their dresses of flowers
Obscuring their gnarled limbs for a season, their wizened branches embrace the gentler breezes of summer
They have a restlessness upon them, some would say elegantly sculptured, they possess an abandonment
The fine gauze of pinky white blossom voices their transient balance with nature, liberating them from the winter drudge
They can be indulgent for a time, beautiful to the eye, daring to be illuminated by primitive, timeless forces, a total completeness
As engraved as their limbs are the ancient ones sigh, in a fragment of time

Hilary Jean Clark

The Birds Are Up

On a cold early evening in January
Just before the sun sets for another day
There's a cry, the birds are up

On the estate where the old folks live
They look through the windows
Some brave the cold venturing outside

But all with one thing in mind
Their eyes look towards the skies
The wonder of nature has begun
There they go, they cry

Starlings, one hundred, two hundred, fill the sky
Until the group is complete
Then they start their mystical dance
Up, down, forming patterns in the sky

What a wonderful sight, nature at its best
Warming themselves for the coming night ahead
On and on they display
And then they return to the land
In which they lay
The birds are down, the sun has gone.

Malcolm J Pettigrew

Light-Draining Spectacular

Slow, steady, soft
outlined by the lazy,
low light.

Filled out on your sofa,
movie on TV
I look over
and your gentle hair
is drawn by the afternoon sunshine.

More than being at the seaside,
air whirling in ears,
rotten seaweed
salty fish smell
sand below me -
more than that,
this is my pleasure.

You, me,
this afternoon
when the light drains spectacular,
watery colours.
I love the days.

Naomi Portman

Rainbows, Christmas Lights, Glows, And Clouds!

Melissa and Jen,
They love to see both the ducks
And rainbow flowers!
On a carriage ride,
The leaves look like Christmas lights!
God is an artist!
Inside the chapel,
Lights have a heavenly glow!
Fall leaves are glowing!
God paints the flowers!
He makes them glow in the dark!
They are Christmas lights!
The flowers of fall,
They glow brighter than the sun,
Both red and orange!
Look at the flowers!
They glow just like red lipstick!
The blue lupines glow!
See the lights outside?
They glow just like golden stars,
A magical scene!
The cottage lights shine,
And there are so many ducks!
I see the fall leaves!
In the summertime,
I enjoy the waterfalls!
They are like soft clouds!
Clockwater Cottage,
The purple leaves surround it.
This is where life starts.

Laraine Smith

What It Means To Be Alive

To shrink, to grow,
To wonder, to know,
To change, to stay,
To stand, to lay,
To hope, to fear,
To go, to come near,
Is what it means to be alive.

To laugh, to cry,
To live, to die,
To work, to play,
To mourn, to be gay,
To touch, to breathe,
To take, to leave,
Is what it means to be alive.

To think, to dream,
To judge, to deem,
To read, to write,
To love, to fight,
To listen, to learn,
To build, to burn,
Is what it means to be alive.

To worship, to adore,
To have less, to want more,
To hug, to kiss,
To live a life of youthful bliss,
To spend, to save,
To have freedom, to be a slave,
Is what it means to be alive.

For all of these feelings on which we thrive,
Is what it means to be alive.

Richard Cannon

October Mere

As I was walking by the Mere
I felt a nippy autumn air
Summer leaves were turning now
Every willow/chestnut bough.

I saw the ducks - each mallard drake
With females bobbing in their wake
And sitting there - all quiet - alone
An angler - was he made of stone?

In the middle - fountain played
Jets of water - surface sprayed
Our pride and joy is fed by springs
Pleasure to South Norfolk brings.

Thus I went my merry way
It was so chilly there to stay
Very much at one - at peace
Life has taken on new lease.

Steve Glason

Lonely Star

On beach of time.
Lie diamonds bright.
On sea of dark
Give eternal light!

In cloak of wisdom
Hide immortal love.
Wrapped in Heaven;
Far up above.

Each one a wonder.
A question why?
Of a life eternal
And time gone by.

That endless suffering.
An empty grave.
A loving soul
That Christ forgave.

Why sparkle, silent
A dream so far.
My loving angel
A shining star.

Anthony Page

Life Of The Dawn

Simple the pleasure
But to walk
In the dawn when the grass is ground underfoot
And to feel the grass
So soft and warm
The sun rays that speak
Of the day to come
And in the dawn
Great cavern sun among the trees
That light its fire as one
And the calling of the crows
That speaks of a new day begun

In the promise of the day
In the glory of the new
Among the charred cinders of the old
Where now stand the chances
Of a better day to be born
Simple the pleasure to see this truth

And in the glory of the new day
Simple the pleasures to see the rising sun
The wakening of the dawn
As it rounds the sky
The calls of the birds
That speak the coming of the light
And fresh and pristine nature in aspic
Newly minted under the new minted light
Of the ever shining sun

Alasdair Sclater

DART Fauna –
The View From My Seat

(Commuting home on the DART - Dublin Area Rapid Transit System)

A man with his glasses
Perched high on his forehead,
As he struggles with the Indo crossword.

The giggling girls in the far seat,
Chatting with iPod in one ear each -
Multitasking.

I can only see the other chap's green cap,
Hovering above his unfolded copy
Of the Irish Times.

Opposite
A girl of about 12 who's reading
'Selected Poems of Carol Ann Duffy'
A bright red beret elegantly pushed back,
On the side of her head.

So, people do still read poetry on the DART!
What a relief!

Mike Wride

Acrostic Poem

R e-invent a Psion
E ndure the past into the future
F or this was a computer organiser
L ight enough to carry in your pocket
E nough thoughtful connotations
C an spark my memory to think
T riumph would be a very great achievement
I n the present, flying through the doors of the past to the future
O f the once sort-after Psion Computer organiser
N ever to fade away again - it is too useful

Josie Lawson

Anything Is Possible

Over the hills and far away
I went wandering one fine day.
The sun was shining oh so bright
I was truly dazzled by its light.

Young and free the whole world before me
Now on my doorstep you'll agree.
What was over the farthest hill?
I was off to see with the strongest will.

I would wander till I found
What was there in that hidden ground.
Would I meet my future love?
Would God look down from far above
And tell me - there lies your fate
The gate is open - go through the gate.
And see what's there for you to find
Be brave, face life with an open mind.

I had no wish to disagree
And luckily you were there for me.
My feet just would not touch the ground
My head - like Earth - was spinning round.

To be loved and then married, what perfect bliss
Like the touch of the sun with its lightest kiss.
The velvet violet, pale primrose and the golden gorse
Are there free for all to see, of course.

Look down while youth is on your side
That gate you walked through was exceptionally wide.
You had courage and with two hands grasped it
From loneliness to marriage, your whole world now is lit.

Jacqueline Bartlett

In Little Moments Of Time

She was bouncing on her trampoline
On a beautiful day outside -
I went to see her.
'Your brother is watching an animated film,
The story of Moses,' I told her.

'Who's Moses?' she said, expressing surprise,
Bouncing, bouncing, bouncing . . .
I laughed at the way she said it.
Seven years old and knowing nothing
About Moses.

She stayed outside, continued to talk
To her grandfather, he was there.
She stayed outside, continued to play,
Leaving her brother to 'The Prince of Egypt'.
She held on to her independent mind.

Her grandfather later told me,
They both talked about this and that,
Freely, in the sunlight.
She was bouncing, bouncing . . .
He asked her, 'What do you want to be

When you grow up?' She thought for herself.
'A good person,' she answered.
It's wonderfully simple.
Just . . . living her life,
And if possible . . . do good.

Claire-Lyse Sylvester

A Lovely Red Rose

I am a lovely red rose
Wet with the morning dew
Waiting for someone to pick me
Hoping that it will be you

I want someone to choose me
Who will like me very much
And think I'm very special
And so very smooth to touch

I want someone to admire me
Who will keep me as their own
And always thinking of me
As the best rose ever grown

But if no one wants me now
I shall fade away and die
My petals will fall around me
And on the ground they will lie

But if I am rejected now
I won't give up and say never
For I will grow again next year
And come back as lovely as ever.

Joan Herniman

Chocolate

Smooth and milky,
You can't beat the taste,
With this particular bar,
There'll be no waste.

A quiet night in,
With no worries at hand,
Eating chocolate,
It's always in demand.

But when it's over,
It's time for a drink,
A glass of water,
Chocolate helps me think.

Jonathan Simms

Too Much Inging

Sunday and I'm free
The papers and a cup of tea
- and me

Monday I'm envisioning
Tuesday is choral singing
Wednesday at a meeting
Thursday I'm rehearsing
On Saturday I'm singing
I'm doing too much inging

But then it's Sunday and I'm free
The papers and a cup of tea
I'm revelling in liberty
Nowhere to go, I can just 'be'
It's just the cat
The BBC
- and me

Margaret Whitehead

Springtime Dawning

To wake up
On a springtime dawn
And see the rising light
Horizon red
The darkness bled
Easing out the night

To stir from sleep
And see the night
Slide gently on its way
Old and tired
Time expired
It greyly fades away

Who knows
What day awaits you
The time that's yet to run
A cloudless sky
And rising high
There's promise from the sun

There's promise
In the dawning
In what there's yet to be
Good or bad
Happy, sad
We have to wait and see

Whatever comes
As day time runs
I'm there and I can cope
What e'er may be
I'll have to see
For I'll have the aid of hope

Ray Ryan

Love

Love Lost

Thank you for the love
That surrounded me
Thank you for the love
That profounded me
Thank you for that nibble
On my ear on a frosty morn
So clear
Thank you for those days
When in love's haze
You and I were so near
Thank you in all ways
For being mine just for
Love's sweet short time.

Robert Walker

Ten Cold Winters

Ten cold winters
Ten cold bended into the sheets and fell asleep
Ten cold winters
Cottages got geriatric, chimneys reeked
Ten cold winters
You were beating me with solid belt
Ten cold winters
I thought that I loved you
Ten cold winters
Barges got frozen, masts stagnated
Ten cold winters
I told the fairy tales and got a birth to the children
Ten cold winters
They found me stagnant and iced in the fisherman's boat
Ten cold winters
The world was waiting for thaw and forgiveness

Rita Valantyte

Close To Your Heart

Tomorrow will you forget me so easily
When I'm no longer there
Close to your heart

Wherever you go
I'll always remember you
When these roads
We're travelling on
Keep us apart

I'll not forget you so easily
Just as long as I have
A beating heart

I'll be wishing I
Was there with you
Wherever you go

When I'm no longer there
Close to your heart.

K Lake

I Love . . .

I love a chocolate milkshake with a Flake,
I hate getting out of bed in the morning,
I love spicy popcorn chicken meals at KFC,
I hate sitting out and watching others having fun,
I love scoring goals when I play football,
I hate the way spiders move,
I love high-tech gizmos,
I hate it when my mum is late picking me up, because I get worried,
I love Forza Motorsport 3 on the Xbox,
I hate lemon, because it is way too sour.

Scott Murrell

Tantra

Bring fruit and candles
Sandalwood is also good
Set a sacred scene
Prepare with care, wash, be clean
On starting tantra use the mantra
Namaste, where we say we want to be one
The ceremony has begun

Eye to eye gazing is amazing
To look and not kiss extends the bliss
By actively resisting each other
We become closer lovers
We give feedback on what repels or attracts
So that before we bond
Our connection is strong, authentic
We've truly meant it

There are no distractions to our interaction
Our kids are asleep
Concentration is deep
We've turned off the phone, so we are alone
All one, a beautiful sum of two parts
Two hearts that cohere, my beloved, my dear

You are Shiva, I am Shakti
Shaking awake our kundalini
Stroking softly with a feather
The arousal is untethered
Together we gather our understanding
Of what the other is demanding in love-making
We're not just hot, we're baking
Our spirits revel in raising sex to the next level

Anna Semlyen

Love

I love my mum, I think she's great!
She's everything you would want,
Although she's always late,
I still love her!

Sometimes she's cross,
Sometimes she's sad,
I still love her!

I love my mum
And she loves me,
She's friendly, pretty and caring.

Sometimes she's winter and angry,
Sometimes she's summer and happy,
I still love her!

She's as lovely as a scarlet-red rose!

May Westcott

Love

My mum is caring, helpful, loving,
She is there for me if I'm hungry,
My mum looks out for me,
If I fall down the stairs or break a bone,
That's why my mum is a hero,
With love!
I love you with all my heart, Mum,
My darling mum,
Love is when someone looks after you,
Like my mum!
She is one and only, beautiful,
Like a blooming lily, that sparkles like a sparkling diamond.

Gemma Lackey

Your Loving Arms

Mine is a frosty noble heart;
The warmth of your love
My heart, alarms!
I become a little child
Lost to your charms.
And then, quite unexpectedly;
This old ice clad frigid heart!
Surrenders softly, thaws and warms,
In the sweet and sultry refuge
Of your tender loving arms.

Keith Miller

False Affection

Touch my lips with your soul.
Hold my hand
let me close my eyes
by your side I'll stand.

I gave you everything
to believe in my return,
return me to my place
I imagined it was by your side.

You promised. You never broke the promise.
Always there, holding me
releasing me. The inner heart believed in you.
You didn't believe in me

Shredding the single idealogy I held
bitter torment through silence.
I thought we loved each other.
Our machine malfunctioned, our pieces didn't fit.

Was I so wrong for loving you?

Alexander Griffiths

A Silent Love

At last, has love lost all its power over me
Here in Alonossos pathos-pathetique
Past connections, lost reactions
Empty sun-soaked passages alight
Like dreams and doves of past delight
Passages of perenatal pressures
Breasted-dimpled pastimes
Far visionary hopes and plans
The warp and weft of hopelessness
Black-bat plans of foolish wishes
Impossible imaginary togetherness
To be love-life-self be free
Only you could take this away from me
The Greek sun and ambiance kisses all away
The chains echo in every sun-sea amplification
Of our silent love starless still in its profound emptiness

Ernest Roberts

With A Kiss

With a kiss it firms the date,
With a kiss it's worth the wait,
With a kiss there's no debate,
With a kiss it's love not hate,
With a kiss it should placate,
With a kiss it's never too late,
With a kiss you've found a mate,
With a kiss it seals your fate.

Geoffrey Leach

Love

Love starts deep within your Being
You probably will not know where
But it is something that you want to Feel
And with others, always hopefully to Share

It will help heal your wounds
It will make your relationships strong
It will uplift your Whole Spirit
It will guide you to right from wrong

Love Permeates your Whole Being
And always makes you feel so good
Why would you shut out Love
Even if you found that you could

It will help show you the way
It will guide you to the right choices
It will sometimes cover you in confusion
It will come to you from other's voices

Love is such a stalwart in life
Through its many varied disguises
Be aware always of its Presence
For sometimes it comes with Lovely Surprises

It will shake you by the hand
It will entwine around your heart
It will fill you with enthusiasm
It will encourage you to make a start

Love is very, very Precious
And comes from Within, from Without, and from Above
So as you Journey along your daily Pathway
Try to base your Every Moment on Pure Love.

Jade Deacon

I Love You Very Dearly

I love you very dearly
But I really must confess
I don't find you attractive
When you sit there in your vest
You sit there watching telly
Then I sit and watch your snore
It's funny when your false teeth
Slip and hit your bottom jaw

You sit and eat your dinner
With a tray upon your lap
But the odd baked bean
Will always seem to somehow find a gap
You never do the dishes
Clean the bath or hoover up
That's women's work you say
As you ask me where's my cup

We don't go out to dinner
To the pictures or the pub
We never see my mother
Cos you can't stand her grub
I often sit and wonder
Why I married you at all
There must have been a reason
I just wish I could recall

I sit and look at you
Out the corner of my eye
You were I must admit once
A very handsome guy
With your hair all long and curly
And your jeans tight on your bum
Perhaps I always knew
That you would be the one

So it doesn't really matter
If you've lost your teeth and hair
Expanded round the waist
And have larger underwear
I'm sure that I will love
Till the stars forget to shine
Or
Does anyone know the number for that new makeover show
You know, the one with what's-'is-name in it?

Lyn Sullivan

Curious Love!

Oh Thrin, dearest Thrin
Y'll always be the Jewel of the South for this poet here,
For, do you recall,
Eight Springs ago, when you two met!
You filled his heart with love in a whim
Sending him far back to his days of youth
Tinted but with the maturity of age
Like a good connoisseur
Knowing of a wine in a cellar dark that's still young and full of prime
Or like an ageless piece of art that's still inspiring and full of life!

Oh Thrin, dearest Thrin,
As you to him
The Jewel of the South you never cease to be
He to you is still his deepest curiosity!

Cornelius Mulvaney

Faithful Wife

The moonlight on a silver sea, an orange sunset sky.
The laughter of a little child, a newborn baby's cry.

Cool water on a summer's day, a sky of deepest blue.
Never were these so lovely as when they were shared with you.

God gave to man, a woman to be his faithful wife
And that is what I'll be to you for all my earthly life.

As from this Holy union we're never meant to part,
The things I love are in His care when Jesus has my heart.

And so I trust in Jesus to hold our love together
I'll be your wife while here on earth and then His Bride forever.

Lesley Mahoney

Lover's Moon

Moonlight softly shining
Sweethearts hand in hand
Reflections on the wavelets
Breaking on the sand
Mystical the moonlight
Magic in the air
Smiling on the lovers
Moonbeams in her hair
Hearts in tune are beating
Was e'er a night like this?
Mystic, magic moonlight
Gentle lover's kiss

Barbara Dunning

You Looked Beautiful Today

I stand here, lost.
You looked beautiful today.
But I was late and missed the moment;
you say it's always the same.
Watching from the sidelines,
I see the rest crumble and fall.
But I remain fighting,
the truth? I refuse to crawl.
I watch the room flood
with the tears of those you loved,
yet wonder who am I to weep;
I shared none of your life's blood.
My thoughts reveal our past
but my memories reveal the lies.
Forcing my way to the front,
standing close, whispering goodbye.
Still I see her screaming, running
from the pain. You meant so much to her:
I hated you taking our life away.
Now as I see her break
fall screaming to the floor,
I remember how much I missed,
how much could have been so much more.

Sunlight settles in the empty air.
I need to run, beg for you to stay.
But who am I to fall?
You looked beautiful today.

Rebecca Bull

See My Love

When can I see my love again?
I have fought battles in anger
It is too much pain for any man
I need to return to where we were

I will look for you in the snowy abyss
The beauty of roses are in your touch
I need nothing more, only this
My sweet love, it is nothing much

Dylan Prins

Devotion

She gives her love with outstretched arms
And kisses fear away,
She tends your wounds
And feeds your growth
And guides you every day.
Mothering her precious young
She protects with her soul,
And loves you with her perfect heart
In the Mother's role.

Linda Knight

Fantasy

He felt it now,
A cold fist kneading at his heart.
The letter in his hand lying crumpled
Like a dead man's skin.
His dream was done.
His super creature was gone.

He had long ago felt that miracles,
Despite all the love he'd given her, had failed.
It was as if she had taken
A knife to her soul,
Carving off slices of feeling
With each cut of the blade.

He had known her secret.
But he'd always dreamt that miracles
Might start functioning,
Might spring up in crimson flowers
And silver stars, proving
That she really loved him.

Sadly, he stepped out of the light
Hugging the darkness to him.
He imagined he heard her voice calling
Her lover's name,
And the thunder of the train departing
Into the increasingly dark night.

He blinked the wetness from his eyes
As he fought the silly, senseless fool thing.
But he still loved her.
No one could love her more.
Shivering, he left the darkness
And slowly closed the door.

Anne Palmer

Untitled

These words are written to congratulate you today
To wish you both love and happiness in a special way
You've found that special someone who leaves that gentle touch
The one and only soulmate for you to love so much
That extra special heart that makes you feel that special way
The one that lives deep inside your heart as love between you grows each day
The one who shares your laughter, your sorrows and your fears
The one who stands beside you as you plan towards the years
So always feel that heartbeat from your soul - deep inside to stay
And cherish all the happiness of your wedding day.

Karen Logan

Beneath The Casement

I linger in the autumn gloom
Where faded memories come and go,
And stare up at the little room
You occupied long years ago.

I mark your passing with a sigh,
And fancy that your ghost lurks there,
Still dreaming where you used to lie,
When you were young and April-fair.

And though the wanton memory sings,
I grieve to think you cannot know
That your soft shade looks out and flings
Sad kisses onto me below.

Stephen H Smith

Sue

Quite some years ago this very day
I never thought I'd feel this way
About a girl that I'd just met
Her name she told me was Jeanette

I soon found out her name was Sue
Who used to paint her eyelids blue
This I suggested she might change
But there's nothing else I'd rearrange

Then as the days and weeks went by
From Christmas time to Valentine's
I fell in love with my girl Sue
She told me that she loved me too

Our love has had its ups and downs
But even when she's not around
More often now I seem to find
She's nearly always on my mind

She means the world and more to me
So now I know there will always be
A place here in my heart for you
My precious, dearest, darling Sue

John Barker

My Wish For You

I've known you now for several years, single, carefree, happy and full of life
Girlfriends came, went, duration varied, one stayed longer, she became your wife
I came to your wedding, wished you well, praying you had made the right decision
You looked so proud that day, on top of the world, but what now, on reflection

I shared your excitement as arrangements went well, suppressinga feeling
of unease
Wary, the relationship apparently dependent on your doing everything to please
You gave it your best shot, she asked, you gave, nothing seemed too much for you
Holidays, sports car, expensive clothes, a puppy, there was nothing you wouldn't do

It was obvious to all, the direction life was taking you, sadly, was all downhill
Totally committed to making it work, the sorry outcome not due to your lack of will
You laughed, joked and smiled outside, but, what about behind the closed door
You never stopped trying to put it back together, the way it was before

As you papered over the cracks, hid true feelings, the pain, it showed in your eyes
Being low, broken-hearted, your world falling about, emotions impossible
to disguise
Now, please try to perceive a new beginning, new places, good times, a new
true friend
Someday she will realise what she has lost, too late, but some broken hearts
never mend

So my wish for you! exciting new life, true happiness, just what you believed
you'd found
But for real this time, someone more mature, a nice little family to turn your
life around
I have no doubt this will come true, your generous, kind nature, will surely make
it right
Love will find you, seize it with both hands, trust your feelings, your future is bright

Morag Grierson

All Of Your Kisses

I like all of your kisses
The happy ones, the sad ones
The tired ones, the blue ones
All of your kisses
The lonely ones, the shy ones
The thrilled ones, the mellow ones
All of your kisses
The fun ones, the tender ones
Even the serious ones

All of your kisses
Written ones, real ones
Murmured ones
Spoken ones
Friendly ones . . .

All of your kisses
Quick ones, little ones
Beautiful kisses
Thank you kisses
Warm kisses, cold kisses
Hurried kisses
Sorry kisses
Close kisses, distant kisses
Worried kisses
Grateful kisses
Inspired kisses

All of your kisses . . .
I like all of your kisses
Beautiful kisses

Georgina Bertin

Goodbye My Love

You didn't hear, you weren't listening
You didn't see the tears glistening
I felt alone, in a wilderness
You didn't ask or try to guess
The pain I felt was so intense
Love conspicuous by its absence

You stared at me through unseeing eyes
A mask in place, on cue faked smiles
I wanted to talk and end the pain
You were unhappy but wouldn't explain
I'd reach for you, you felt so cold
Everything's OK my heart I told

But I knew I'd lost you somehow, somewhere
I knew you'd fought to pretend you care
Why did the truth take so long to say?
I knew in time you would go away
My heart went with you, I'm incomplete
Just waiting for the day we'll once again meet

Barbara Lambie

I Love And Hate

I love my mum, she helps me with my homework,
I hate it when I'm dirty after I've played around in the wet,
I love it when the sun shines bright,
I hate it when my grandad tickles me,
I love the birds when they sing the morning hymn,
I hate it when I have to clean out my pets,
I love it when it's raining and sunny, it makes a beautiful rainbow.

Chloe McArthur

Love In The Morning

In the silence of the morning
I turn and watch you sleeping
I lay my head upon your chest
and breathe in your essence
as your eyelids flicker
you stir and pull me close

You gently open your eyes
no words are needed
you kiss my forehead gently
and lull me back to sleep

I wake again but you are gone,
your fragrance lingers on my pillow
and your love lingers in my heart
I smile to myself for I am happy
saved by your love . . .

Paula Greene

Angel

Angel my soul is on fire
Burning with thoughts of passion and desire
I see deeper than the bluest of seas
Feel more deeply, see, I have the keys
The privilege is more than I can humanly bear
Sometimes, something of a nightmare
However, to share it openly with you
Enriches me with shades and colours of every hue
To feel . . . and see . . . and know
Is like a Gift, with . . . an elaborate bow

Ivana Cullup

What Is Love?

Love, what is love? So difficult to define,
Heady, like floating in the air, and wine,
Nectar of the gods, golden, shining through the glass
We would be fools to let it pass.

Love lives in a different fascinating world,
High above the clouds, looking down, and hurled
Into a wonderland of captivating dreams,
Does it promise what it seems?

Yes, if we nurture it with tenderness and so,
Cradle it in our arms and never let it go,
As we look at the stars shining in the skies,
A sense of wonderment is reflected in our loved one's eyes.

Love will last forever and forever,
Nothing in this world, or the next, can sever
The bonds of love and its attendant mystery,
As shown through countless years of history.

Irene Greenall

You

You brightened my life for a short while
You made me smile, laugh and giggle
We played games with each other
I felt young again, as though I were a mere 17
I was excited, playful, flirtatious, teasing as well as sparkling
Looking forward in unpredictable anticipation
And then,
Disillusionment, realisation of a specific genus

Sasch Bainbridge

Sonnet For Shashi

Let me be your hero with sword in hand
Your metaphorical knight in armour.
At your beck and call, always your command,
Epitome of the perfect charmer.
Let me worship you, let me sing your psalm,
Let me whisper sweet nothings in your ear.
Let me hold you close in these trembling arms,
And breathe in your aroma when you're near.
In your eyes there's beauty beyond compare
In your smile, the warmth of a summer's day
Each kiss is a statement to which I swear,
That I love you more than mere words can say.
Let us be star-crossed lovers, you and me,
And walk hand in hand through love's mystery.

Keith Tissington

Deep Blue

Your eyes are like the sea deep blue
Another thought will make me yearn
I swam in love and drowned for you
Your eyes are like the sea deep blue
A chance to hold and float with you
A risk I took and hoped to learn
Your eyes are like the sea deep blue
Another thought will make me yearn

Adrian Horton

Love Is A Rose

Love is a red rose that perpetuates colours of beauty
It always fulfils its duty
That grows from bushes and weeds in the green meadows that
Promoting the healing of heart before we drift apart
So precious to our life blood
Its vulnerability screams out all the love
Creating peace between our hearts
Answering our very wish
A sentimental moment for us to see, feel and treasure
In a plantation where memories are sewn
Where trust and love grows between us
The buds of spring shall follow
The rose begins to bloom on its throne, as the journey becomes
An infinite abode signifying warm winds of tomorrow and
Cold winds of yesterday when old things pass us by
Like the fate of a growing rose in the grass
We cry for peace and solidarity that is the emblem of the rose that lasts
Which guides us and keeps us united and our sorrows at bay
The rose becomes our uniform and mascot
So strong; left standing in luscious fields with bluebells and poppies
That liberate bees and butterflies at play
Where birds in the trees sing their sweet praise and the whispering winds of mercy
Still scatter the innocent tender seeds of change
Protecting the secret of life that lies in the eye of a bud, nurtured underground in
the mud
Through the darkness comes hope from rays of sun that splash out on a sunny day
Euphoria soon dissipates as in the golden garden the seeds are dispersed
And some are lost by the water hose
Waiting for beautiful shades of colour to sprout inside
No one knows its secrets yet to be exposed as
Sentimental memories come flooding back when I approach
The smell of a special rose left standing motionless like my frozen emotions
I awake to another sweet day unable to repel the seduction of the smell
Love takes on many forms found in places where we dwell
The smells that emanates from the romantic rose give our true emotional
entwinement
That remains fertile fragile and enclosed
Like the bud that slowly decomposes from a wounded stem

That is devastated by a broken heart
On one velvet rose, each petal is sacrificed from
The tender stem, by an insensitive lover's touch
Which her fingers and shadows of her loving gaze encompass
With salty tears, she cuts the rose stem that quivers
And feels vulnerable to the pouring rain so delicate and in pain
The sick rose suffers in the cold as winter unfolds
The sad rose head is hiding the joy of life as it looks out
To the pouring rain for tomorrow's domain
Only time makes the rose begin to droop and fade away
There is nothing left to face but freedom
In another environment while conditions are mildly favourable
Time elapses it adapts each day it has no choice
But to stay and pray for the short journey it has on Earth
The artificial life in the vase, persecutes the gentle head
With all the strain the stem becomes weak and irritated it sheds its leaves
Until the flower diminishes, struggles and ceases to breathe
Devoted and hopelessly in love, withering and isolated it dies in time while
another rose opens and grows in the garden outside.

Nassira Ouadi

Embrace Me

Embrace me with your eyes for everywhere
I look, I hear your sighs surround my soul,
Like star beach wavelets hies that oceans stir,
Like cosmic's deep that laps skies lucent bowl,
There yearnings call transcends night's all enthrall,
To ebb and flow in love's devouring bliss,
And shore the heavens covered with heart's pall,
With whispered, 'Miss yous' sweetest star bright kiss
Yet in this some light tide of photon hush,
Disquiet is my rush that mirrors there,
While hopes like fountain cascades raindrop gush,
With longing that no longings ever bare,
Thus as stars aqua Valentine in love,
Will this cusp see swell seeing see my dove?

Barry Bradshaigh

The Meaning Of Love

Who can define love?
Too wide, too deep to be trapped in a word.
It has no boundaries, no limitations.
Love pours from the heart like a bottle of wine that never empties.
Eyes meeting like stars across a black sky: twinkling, twinkling;
A secret smile, tears of joy or sadness with no need of words;
Sharing a wondrous view from a hilltop
With a squeeze of a hand and a feeling of awe;
Watching the sunset together lighting up the skies
With an explosion of colour from God's paintbox: changing, changing;
Feelings of joy filling both hearts with rapture, ecstasy.
Love is the embrace, the entwining, the magic of desire
Burgeoning like springtime or the awakening of dawn;
Kiss sealed, bliss secured, blessed by God;
Passion's flames lit in ultimate togetherness;
With senses heightened, a lightness of foot on rose-petalled paths;
Caressing, possessing, expressing commitment, never letting go;
A warmth of mind, body and spirit:
Spreading, spreading;
Lighting the soul with the unimaginable serenity of love.

Janet Lang

Sleeping Angel

A calmness falls over the room, your breathing eases as I stroke your neck,
My fingers glide gently over the tiny golden hairs.

The steady rhythm of our music lulls the atmosphere into calm,
Your hands drop from my waist,
And I watch your face turn to form a peaceful expression.
I place my palm on your chest,
To feel your steady heartbeat as I mould myself around your sleeping figure.

My alert mind gives into the relaxing air,
And I slip into an unconscious serenity.
As I wait to be awakened by your glowing life;
That lights my darkest day.

James Blackwell

The Dream

(Dedicated with love to Julia who so enriched my life by being in it)

She walks, with beauty in the velvet night
footsteps soft as a petal's fall
a fragrance, gentle as a summer breeze
that whispers secrets through the leafy trees
scents the air as she passes by . . .
A touch, feather light as a thistledown . . .
a bluebell tinkle of laughter, then . . .
she is gone,

and yet . . . her presence lingers still
the coolness of her fingers in my hand
restores my heart and mind, and . . .
in that deep, abiding love I find that we
can never part.

Harry Pryce

Don't Let Anything Come Between Us

When each day passes by
When every hour passes by too
I'm unconditionally thinking of you

Do not let the ocean divide us
Do not let the language cause a barrier
A barrier of love.

When I see you again
I will never, I will never
I will never let you go
Let the difference in culture bring us together.

Do not let the ocean divide us
Do not let the language cause a barrier
A barrier of love.

If I did not call you
If I do not hear your voice
My tears would just keep on flowing
If I saw you face to face
I would fall into your arms.

Let's make the impossible possible
Because our love for each other
Has just grown and grown.

Robert Bradley

Those Moments

You looked at me . . . your eyes spoke volumes
But you only said good day
We were separated by language and culture
But love showed us the way.
Your touch spoke to me
Of ecstasy and bliss
And oh, the doors that opened
In the magic of your kiss.
As we gazed deeply into each other's eyes
The world became ours . . . it's true
Nothing mattered but those moments
Those moments that we shared, we two.

Joyce Hudspith

Our Love

Our love is Spring,
Heralding the promise it can bring,
Nurtured with tenderness and care,
Blossoming to joys beyond compare.

Our love is Summer,
Held in warm embrace,
All happiness and laughter -
No tears bedew its face.

Our love is Autumn,
Discarding dying dreams,
Only truth laid bare,
Its strength our hope -
Whatever our despair.

Our love is Winter,
All passions rage, until
The storm is spent,
Leaving us the stillness
Of deep and sweet content.

Beryl Andrews

One Romantic Night

We graced the dance floor
Close in each other's arms
We swayed to the waltz
Your laughter and voice
A melodious symphony of sound
I clung to your body replete in our embrace
Wishing mine would melt into yours
I love your hair,
Your earlobe, and face
I am tempted to trace, but I settle
For the graceful curve of your neck
As I place on it a loving kiss
I breathe in your scent
Not of the aftershave but of you
You gaze into my eyes and I'm in Heaven
I am not afraid to express my love
Because we have been made one
The soothing music and the candlelit room
Destabilise my senses
I can feel your body next to mine
Virile and alive as we share a kiss
Whilst continuing to dance into the night

Debra Valley

Falling In Love

The wonderful experience of falling in love,
It can happen when old, middle age, or young;
Instantly romantic and exhilarating is the way,
From that day on your life will change.

Some say it does not happen instantly,
That sort of dull thinking will not do for me;
The explosion of falling in love is a feeling,
Now is the time for its revealing.

You have to have the chemistry,
If you are to be in ecstasy;
It does not take long to make a dream come true,
I know it is an experience I have been through.

She is hot and all in flushes,
His legs are gone and in need of crutches;
The heart has a sudden rushing beat,
In a minute the process is complete.

In an hour your head still in a daze,
Life together is the only way;
Now you have Spring fever,
How can you ever leave her?

Of all the things in God's creation,
Falling in love is an extraordinary sensation;
It took a million years of creation to make all those stars you now see above,
But it only takes a minute to fall in love.

Robin Robinson

Romeo

Perched on the seat not coming too close
My internet Casanova came to me
Eating muffins and drinking tea
My internet Casanova came to me
Well he looked like his photo
His accent drove me wild
Dearest One you are here with me
Yes, Romeo is drinking tea
Computer shut down, mouse on hold
A kiss might not have been bold
Maybe one day our lips might meet
Until then, drink your tea
My internet Casanova came to me.

Jessie Shields

Latent Love

I thought to tell you my love,
What latent love could be;
For gentle kisses that caress your cheeks,
Could smoother be

I gave you love, and happiness too,
To you I opened my heart;
Mistrusting, blank, in heavenly fears,
Ah, you did depart!

When you were gone from me,
A flaming star came by;
Smoothly, softly, in deep admiration,
He took me with a sigh.

Shamim Ruhi

Love's Journey

I've felt the pain of lost love,
As deep as any sword,
When a careless heart has broken
Love's umbilical cord.

Felt abandoned as a kitten
Left out in the snow;
Cold, and desolate and lost
With no warm place to go.

Then the dearest, kindest man
Came into my life,
Wanting one thing only;
For me to be his wife.

We've now been married forty years
Contented still in love,
Like a foot to a comfy slipper
Or a hand to a well-used glove.

Now settling into later life
By the firelight's soft glow
I sometimes think of those old loves
And the heartache long ago.

Then I look at the one that endured,
The love that was meant to be,
Knowing till death I'll be there for him
As he will be there for me.

Shirley Brooks

Samson And Delilah

The ultramarine sea was reflected
in the eyes of the girl
who sat dreaming on a rock,
it was about her lover whose
red gold hair sprang and coiled
like the contents of Pandora's Box.

She saw him coming along the path
his body outlined against the evening sun,
he kissed her passionately then sat beside her.
taking scissors from her bag
she began to cut his hair.

A blood-red sun was setting
when the last curl was shorn.
The girl looking ethereal
flings the red gold curls into the sea,
they fall like drops of blood
disturbing gulls who scream their protest.

Sighing he feels his hedgehog stubble
and has a moment of regret
but she throws her arms around him
pressing her lips against his
overcome by her touch
he feels his strength ebbing
his eyes become like dark pools
reflecting twilight's bruised sky.

Rosaleen Clarke

An Old Man's Darling

Some say it's better for a girl who seeks
experience with love before marriage
to comfort an old man's somewhat bleak
last years, as his heart's hansom carriage.

With a wealthy squire, that phase is superb.
Money is spent more frequently on treats -
outings and gifts, whose value may perturb
less free-thinking folk she meets on home streets.

So many women marry later, now.
They want to have achieved some of their dreams,
which husbands, often, curtly disallow.
With their love, nobody needs life's extremes.

Gillian Fisher

The Reason

Not even when I saw her face
Not when you created distance
Not when my ankle snapped
Not with your verbal attack
Not with your cold shoulder
Not with their words of anger
Not when you left me with the shame
Not when you let me take all the blame

My feelings for you never waived
My emotions for you never changed
This is the reason I can never see you again.

P Dixon

Just A Memory

When the harbour's surrounded
By its myriads of lights,
And ships stand silhouetted
'Neath a moon shining bright.
When the wind howls no longer
Clouds so gently sail by,
Forming shapes quite fantastic
In a vast, boundless sky.
When water laps gently
All is calm and serene,
I will stand and recapture
What seems now like a dream.

It is moments like that, which
Make one's life worthwhile,
For my heart filled with pleasure,
On my lips was a smile.
Whilst you stood there beside me
Of my thoughts unaware,
I asked God to watch o'er you
With His Own Loving Care.
And where'er you may travel,
On the land or the sea,
May the 'good' things life holds
Be forever with thee.

Esther Hawkins

Turkish Delight

Holiday romances
Are bound to be taboo,
But ours was like a fairy tale
When I fell in love with you.

Our love was fully tested,
The differences to blame,
Completely different cultures,
Our language not the same.

Overwhelming obstacles
Seemed to block up every lane
The only thing we understood
Was one another's name.

Couldn't have a conversation,
But didn't seem to care.
At first, we must have seemed
The oddest loving pair.

Ours is quite a story,
Written in its part
The title is quite simple
Eye to Eye: Heart to Heart.

Farina May Jenkins

Romance

For years and years I dreamt of
A man on a fine white horse
Cantering down the North Circular Road
Perchance he was well off course.

Coming to carry me away
To a life in a far-off land
But now he'll need a forklift truck
Cos my weight's got out of hand.

Oh, the dreams we had when we were young
The sights we were going to see
Imagine a knight in shining armour
Coming to Neasden just for me.

It doesn't hurt to sleep and dream
Of love and great romance
It doesn't happen much in real life
Not too many get that chance.

But I still dream of romance
Cos life can be a bit boring
Lying next to my old man
Listening to him snoring.

So as I sleep and dream at night
I can still see that white steed
Galloping down the fast lane
With a fair turn of speed.

But he always goes past Neasden
Which isn't a lot of fun
So in my sleep I wave goodbye
As he gallops up the M1.

Dorothy Fuller

The Loss Of A Loved One's Love!

As we journey on the road of life
With loving kith and kin
So many things just seem to come
Disturbing peace within.

And many times the blows just hurt
The pain won't go away
And those we dearly love and trust
Don't hear the words we say.

The flame that once burned deep within
Has flickered right away
Yet in our hearts, we know it's there
- may loved ones feel it, pray.

Remembering now such happy times
And seeking them again
My prayer to you, my Saviour King
- Please, take away my pain.

Please bring me back my own dear love,
And let us know again
The peace and love we shared so long,
Please take away our pain.

Anne Gray

Half Of My Whole

(For Steve)

You were my sunshine, my laughter, my rain
You were the balm that soothed all my pain
You would be there when I needed a friend
I thought you'd be with me until my life's end
You kept me safe always there when I called
You were the half of my whole

Our love was sacred, our love was strong
We stuck together when things did go wrong
We shared our secrets, we shared our life
We were so happy to be man and wife
As the memories I sadly recall
For you were the half of my whole

You gave me comfort and calmed all my fears
You were the one there to dry all my tears
I truly believe we were meant to be
Though what laid ahead I could never foresee
You made my heart sing, gave wings to my soul
Now you are gone, I can never be whole.

Margaret Martin

Trapped Butterflies

Craziness unfurling
from somewhere beyond
the love that's inside
has not died

Temptation's hurting
although it's so wrong
the feelings inside
won't subside

Emotions erupting
they need to explode
the passion inside
I can't hide

Thoughts corrupting
all parts of my mind
a life-changing choice
to decide

Stomach's churning
from butterflies within
I feel there inside
but can't fly

Tension's stirring
from the chemistry there
whirling inside
but deprived

Paola Borella

Dream On Olden

My work is done and dusted,
And now I'm on my way.

To call in at my local,
To end another day.

I have a friend, who works there,
She's very pretty with fair hair.

A lovely body I can see,
I only wish she was with me.

Her name is Jo, I'll have you know,
Her age it matters not.

I'll stop a while to see her smile,
Then be on my way.

Forty years too old I am,
To tempt the likes of Jo.

But I live in dreams like old men do,
Till it's time to go.

B J Shire

Angels Are Rare

Sing to me softly sweet song of bird
Sweetest of music that ever was heard
Lips like petals on bud of a rose
Softer lips on no other grows

Rest upon me those bold seeing eyes
Make my spirits soar to the skies
Feel I'm nowt but a miserable worm
When I gaze upon your heavenly form

Never a man's heart beat so fast
Never a man so breathless gasp
Angels are rarely ever seen
That's why I hold you in high esteem

I've bared to you my heart, my soul
Stand and tremble like a newborn foal
When will this quake in me subside?
My guess is only when this life dies

A home in Heaven a Christian finds
Though it breaks my heart leave you behind
In those years ahead, in life anew
I'll keep a sharp lookout, waiting for you

Arthur S Waller

The Beauty Of Her Precious Lips

The beauty of her precious lips
Can take my breath away -
I tingle to my fingertips
And can't think what to say!
I blurt out words that don't make sense
And folly breaks love's spell!
Perhaps one day we can be friends,
But only time will tell . . .
I pray to God for some advice -
I can't do this alone.
Although I've got to break the ice,
Such skills I've never known.
To say, 'I love you!' right out loud,
That's quite beyond me now!
I've never stood out from the crowd,
So God must help somehow!
The beauty of her precious lips . . .
Yes, I know what bliss is!
In my romantic daydreams trips,
She's the Queen of Kisses!
I know I'm not the kind of guy
To sweep her off her feet,
But love deserves a second try
With someone who's so sweet . . .
If she's the one I'm meant to wed,
I'd like God on my side
Until our Wedding vows are said,
When I may kiss my bride . . .

Denis Martindale

Poetry In Motion

I will make you strong when you feel weak
I will be the inspiration behind every single heartbeat
I will be the helping hand that pulls you back upon your feet

When you feel hungry, I shall be the food you eat
Even when I am gone, I will always be so near
When you feel scared, I will take away your fear

When you feel angry, I will calm and soothe you
When you feel hurt, I will be your pain relief
When you feel tired, I shall help you sleep
I shall be the oxygen that will make you breathe

I will give you all the love you need
When you feel down, I will give you hope
I shall always be there for you when no one else is around
If your heart is broken, I will mend it piece by piece

I will wipe away your tear before it falls upon your cheek
I will be the spirit that you feel deep down in your soul
I will show you respect and appreciation
I shall value your true worth

I shall be your destiny to make your life complete
I will do all these things for you and so much more
If only I could have you back again
In my life once more . . .

Annette Foreman

All Of My Heart,
A Love Sonnet

I'll give you all my love,
to you all of my heart
upon a silver platter
I give it all to you!

Let me hold your hand,
so very tight as we walk
both taking the pathway of romance
that shines with stars of love.

As I look deep into your eyes,
I see two flames before me
like two lamps amidst the darkness
the very light of true love.

And my desire is to kiss you,
upon your ruby-red lips
to hold you so very tightly
and to never let you go!

I'd give you all of my heart,
this day to truly bless
hearts that would beat as one
in unison with the rhythm of love!

Simon Foderingham

My Wish For You

(A sonnet)

Our lives consist of past memories,
present happenings,
and future hopes.
I trust your past has many more memories
of joy rather than of sorrow,
and the happenings of the present
will add to the joyous memories of your past.
As to the future, who knows
what that has in store.
I can only hope, when your future
becomes the past,
you have had many days of laughter
and just a few occasions for tears
which were rapidly dispelled.

John Willmott

Body Language

An entanglement of legs and arms
enclosing emotions,

Soft skins meeting adding to
soft words spoken,

Tongues touching, teasing parts
Trying to express the hidden heart,
When the sighs and moans are repressed

Preventing utmost pleasure to be expressed.

Viv Fitzpatrick

Understanding Love

Love shall find as love shall seek,
Favour hides from Fear and Weak,
Romance knocks not at your door,
But calls to venture forth, explore.

Hesitant to start anew,
Love can blindly miss its cue,
To worship shyly from afar,
Apart, under same fated star.

Love possessed, belongs elsewhere,
Denies our souls to meet and share,
Love draws back, so Cupid's dart
Shall not reward deserving heart.

Pride withholds our heart and hand,
Destroys what we don't understand,
Or can't control; then love must die,
Or worse, unknown, continue by.

Val Haslam

Reality's Rainbow

We walk hand in hand, my love and I - so close,
Whilst in my heart, I feel only sad and morose.
I mourn for the precious love we threw away -
I wish that it would return again to stay!

We had a dream, the two of us, which now is gone.
A dream of togetherness, of hope, of joy that shone
Like the pot of gold at the rainbow's end,
So broken now, I fear it will never mend.

Perhaps it was too fragile ever to last,
Reality intrudes on make-believe cruelly fast,
Bringing the realisation life holds less joy than sorrow -
Yet keeping us yearning for that bright tomorrow!

Lorena Valerie Owens

Love

Love, love is the greatest gift
We can share
Without love, there is no care
Without love, it would be just me
And not you,
For with love, I share with you,
My love is no longer with me,
But in the arms of love himself,
God above,
True love never dies
But lasts for eternity
As it has been said,
'Better to have loved and lost
Than never to have loved at all'.
Love, love is the greatest gift of all
Through God's love, we came into being
And He gave us love,
So we could share and care for one another,
Jesus' love has us free,
Because He went to Calvary
And died upon the tree,
Because only His blood could set us free.

Stanley John Moore

Silly Words

I would love to write a poem about the love and the tenderness,
I would love to write of that warm feeling and sensation of safety,
I would love to sit in a dizzy haze of happiness,
I would love to be loved again,
I would love to write a poem about being loved by you.

I would love to write a poem about laughing out loud,
I would love to write about the heartfelt sound,
I would love to hold my sides from the aching laugh,
I would love to write a poem about laughing with you.

I would love to write a poem about being with you again,
I would love to write about holding onto you tight,
I would love to sit beside you, there was no need for words,
I would love to love you again,
I would love to write a poem about you.

I would love to write a poem about missing you so,
I would love to write about that ache that remains here still,
I would love to tell you all that I never did tell,
I would love to be living with you again,
I would love to write a poem just for you . . .
But, I can't, as,
All I have,
Are these silly . . .
Words . . .

Della Perry

Forbidden Love

You walked into my life and
Turned it upside down.
It hit us like a whirlwind
That first day you came around.

No awkwardness, no silences,
Everything felt right.
Alone at last, you sat beside me
Well into the night.

Can I kiss you, is what you asked,
Looking deep into my eyes.
I wanted you to stay forever,
No more goodbyes.

Your lips touched mine, so soft
And warm and wow!
An electric shock surged through
My body, straight into my heart
Pow!

You took me in your arms, it felt
So warm, safe and true.
Our bodies trembled with desire,
I really wanted you.

I had never felt such pleasure, as
Your hand brushed against my breast.
You felt it too, your body tensed,
Yet we both held back with zest.

J Pope

Sweet Dreams

You're the one I've been looking for all my life,
Now we've hooked up, we can live the high life,
I've bucked up my ideas, want you as my wife,
I've stopped chucking up beers, you get me high,
Like a sky dive, to beer I've said bye,
Sick of feeling dead, time to feel alive,
Let the good times roll, I could eat you whole,
I'm on top of the world, I'll take the lead role,
You tantalise my tastebuds, taste so good,
I'll embrace the love, stop being wasted on drugs,
I want to sample life without being hungover,
Feel good sober without being drunk in a coma,
Smell coffee's aroma, you're my shoulder to cry on,
When nights are colder, you're the one I can rely on,
After a hard day's work, I can't wait to see you,
In your arms, out of harm's way, girl, I need you.

Girl, you're a real charmer, make me feel calmer,
Like I'm sat under palm trees in the Bahamas,
With a calm breeze, mind at ease,
Drinking wine, sharing Chinese,
These feelings I have, make me want to grab you,
With both hands, I'm so glad you,
Walked into my life, I talk about you all the time,
You're there for me when I fall out of line,
You care for me, you call me every break time,
I'm turned on when you flex your waistline,
To T's bass lines, we're going to have a great time,
Have a late night drinking snake bites,
I give you a rose as a token of my love,
As you chose me, you got me to open up,
It's so good, I knew I'd hit the jackpot,
When I laid eyes on you, you're no crackpot.

Girl! I want to show you off to the world,
You rock my world, put me on top of the world,
You float my boat, a long soak in the tub,
Champagne, oysters, smoking the bud,
You grope me good, girl! It's us forever,

Together, we're tougher than leather,
For better, for worse and if it gets err worse,
I'll stick by you, any debts, threats or curse,
I'll put you first, let's make music like Chopin,
I hope I'm still with you when I'm an old man,
I love you truly, deeply, dearly, madly,
I'd do anything for you, I need you badly,
I want to be your companion for life,
I'll carry on until you're my wife,
There's no comparison, with my last girlfriend,
Embarrassing, harassing, but you get 10 out of 10.

James Hazell

Darling My Love

Darling my love, I will give to you
Knowing that your love is really true
Darling you know that I'll give my all
Yes, all I will give when you do call

Each time I see your smiling face
My heart beats faster as in a race
I know I still love you with all my heart
That's how I felt right from the start

You know that I love you
You know it is true
I've loved no other but only you
So darling tell me you still love me

Ray Duncan

Sweet Sixteen

At sweet sixteen I'd heard so much about this thing called 'love' -
They said it dropped into your life and gave your world a shove . . .
They said, 'You'll feel delighted; that skies would all be blue
And every hour of every day I'd want to spend with you . . .'

They said you'd gaze into my eyes and whisper words so true
And I would fall beneath the spell - of you, simply being 'you'!

They said we'd dream and plan and scheme and love our whole lives through
And there'd be nothing in the world I would not do for you.

They never warned of sleepless nights when you didn't even phone
When I'd have wild imaginings whilst sitting home - alone . . .
They never warned of 'someone else', trying to steal your heart.
Doing her best, with her female charms, to prise our souls apart . . .
So, by the time that I was seventeen, I began to appreciate
That the wear and tear and the price you pay
Is too high for a loving mate!

Edna Sparkes

Blind Love

I am so sorry that I ever doubted your love
I am sorry that I pushed you away
I would not hold you in my arms
I snubbed your kisses
I acted cruelly
I never believed a word you said
I could not see into your heart
To know you spoke the truth
I could not see myself adored in your eyes
I was blind until it was all far too late
And I did not notice love until I lost you.

Pamela McCormack

Troubled Soul Forever Seeking

To see what you have missed for most of your life
I witness beauty and thank fate for being so kind
A cycle of loving thoughts enter the mind
Though I often feel scared
With worries and fear
I thank someone that you are here
My heart reaches out, often confusion comes from the mouth
Though we never met we have our special dance
Entranced by the energy that realised my inner glow
Surprised by my words often truly felt
When you feel near the earth falls from under
I wonder about
Dismayed without you I long to touch you
Others may try to steal you away
I know my sweet that I shall have my day
The world will stop the heavens be open
I have waited so long with such devotion
Awaiting the hour when we both see the same stars
A perfect moment
Feel our pleasure
Let us float to the sky and yonder on high
As a bird feels free when we meet you can unravel me
With patience
With my usual fear
I await you dear

Louis Cecile

True Love

Each time I close my eyes, I think of you, my love
My thoughts for you are higher than the clear blue sky above
You are with me now
Deep in my heart
Although we are apart
The happiness you give to me
Will last for evermore
Each time you say you love me
It is greater than before
Your thoughtfulness and honesty
Shine like the morning sun
The way you kiss me like our love has first begun
When you look into my eyes so tenderly
I know how much you love me
When you hold my hand
I know how much you care
We have a love so strong
So true, a love that we share
We have a love I can't describe
No words I can compare.

Isabel Taylor

A Whole Lot Of Love

(Dedicated to my soulmate, my husband George, with love)

There's so much love between us,
So many wonderful feelings,
Love is . . . butterflies in the stomach,
Love is . . . going wobbly at the knees,
Love is . . . feeling like you're walking on air,
Love is . . . goosebumps when you see each other,
Longing to be together,
Feeling half a person, only whole again,
When you have your loved one near.

These feelings are so lovely,
And you feel so very strong,
So then being in love with that special someone,
Is never, ever wrong,
It makes loving someone special,
So worthwhile,
And certainly brings a great big smile.

Sara Jane Berry

Love

The total left over
From another
With retrospect,
Left to correct
With little touches,
Accents and decorative
Ornaments
As if meant
To give only
And live completely.

Nicola Barnes

You Rescued Me

You rescued me
From a woeful existence
You lifted me out of the grey clouds
You lit up my life
When you asked me to be your wife
You showed me blue skies
And how to live
I'll never look back
To my past miserable life
Cos now I am happy
Now I'm your wife
You showered me with gifts
Of your love
And jewels so delightful
You make me feel good
And showed me life as it should be . . .
You rescued me!

Theresa Hartley-Mace

Untitled

As I sit and look at him across from me, I feel the intensity
As he touches me, I feel my soul move with every stroke
As I hear the words he speaks, I feel uncertainty
As we make love, wait is it love?

Krista Kauffman

First Love

I distinctly remember when in my teens
I wore winkle pickers and faded blue jeans
Testosterone rising, like some raging bull
Constantly looking for someone to pull
Despite all the plotting and all the schemes
I'd still to meet the girl of my dreams
When out of the blue, one day on the tram
Our eyes did meet, my heart went wham!
Beehive blonde, beguiling smile
The tastiest bird I'd seen, by a mile
Hourglass figure, emerald-green eyes
Great three-penny bits and thunder thighs
With her cashmere sweater and short mini-skirt
She blew bubblegum and started to flirt
I plucked up courage to ask for a date
To which she accepted and said, 'Don't be late!'
Destined to meet, never to part
Cupid's arrow straight through my heart.

Ian Tomlinson

Boundless Ocean

Loving thee is like throwing pebbles in the sea,
Your power is all-consuming, it overwhelms me.
Your love it washes over and cleanses me anew,
My thoughts are all of thee, and my heart I give to you.

'To know the love of Christ, which passeth knowledge, that ye
might be filled with all the fullness of God'. Ephesians 3 v 19.

Melanie Biddle

Babylon

The gates of Aztec, with platinum bolts,
The hieroglyphics engraved
As I entered, the dream began,
My glory of the life in Babylon
The smell of jasmine, the essence of thyme,
The blossomed tulips that rise so high,
The vines that entwine around pillars of gold
And the scrolls that tell tales of new and old.
The palace is flawless, with spiral staircase with pearl,
The guardians that guard the walls so tall,
The spears were thin and the blade of Sparta so sharp,
As the bards sing of it, playing their harps.
The voices of peace and harmony
Echoed amongst the marble stone,
Water comes down from mountain crops
Surrounding women in their silky tops.
I, myself, have nothing to regret,
I must have Glory, if I don't then why?
I have something now, a prize to collect
That I can either claim or buy.
The room was filled with all colours so free,
Ebony, silk and ivory, a jackpot of three,
And my companions and I each have a key
For the pleasures of a lifetime that lie ahead for me.
The day passed by and the sun came down,
The lights were dimmed and the curtains drawn,
The bed was open, rose petal gown
Within a second her dress was down,
She pulled my robe and it filled the floor,
Her breasts so soft, silken smooth,
My lips touched hers, as my hands made their move,
As I stroked her, she whispered for more.
It felt like love at first touch,
My heart was beating so fast,
I wanted her more and more,
If only this could last.

The morning was pleasant, the breeze so free,
The swallows sang in the orchid tree,
I may look frightening, but there's no need to flee,
Once you penetrate my armour, you shall see the true me.

The life here is sweet Babylonian balm,
The clouds that sleep so quiet and calm,
This woman's presence is not all that it seems,
When the muses sing, feather-like life fills my dreams.
The water so pure, like true love's first kiss
Our witness of love, the god Aphrodite
Together we write this poem of bliss
As our steps lead us into matrimony.

Ben Jones

A Reminder To Love

For a few short weeks when my father passed away
There was a will to behave with decency.
We all made an effort and spoke quite earnestly
Of the things we'd do, my mother, my brother and me;
Yet it turned out we were doomed by history.

Or perhaps we were mainly undermined by fear:
Was my mother scared she'd suddenly disappear?
That without Dad, people would find her dull,
Her way of living too conventional?
For whatever reason, she decided to kick up hell.

Her behaviour resembled that of an alley cat
Cultivating affection, then dropping you flat.
Her stories figured herself in the victim's role,
She went off crying wolf to her male siblings;
And in this way, felt loved and protected again.

Although most of the harm was done to herself,
And abandoning daily calls was some relief,
For a time I was really consumed with grief.
Surely we're fools to waste what love remains?
As this poem is to remind me, when I'm her age.

Ann Watson

Little Beloved

I dreamed of her the night before
A cry from the shade
And a living, beating part of me
The next day she asked
Can I come?
No
I said
Let the dust settle
Couldn't you come back another time?
Your timing is terrible
Your father cannot see me
He loves only minstrels
And I made big plans
For my important future
And your timing . . .
Would you love my son?
Now it seems I carried my children
On opposite sides
I lie like a foetus in the tub
With the curtains pulled around
And try to be near you
You can't talk to me can you?
You are too little

Often you will hover
Above my red, torn scalp
Tap-tapping from both sides
Let me in
That day I tore you
From your soft red pillow
9am on a stark autumnal morning
Fat citrus tears formed
Ready to drop
Every September

Katherine Beaumont

You Are

You are the love of my life
And I won't let you go
Sometimes my emotions get the best of me
And they come in tides until they overflow

I know you love me
And your love will stay true
No matter how much I act like I don't care
I only care for you

You came into my life unexpectedly
I've always known you were the one
I find comfort knowing that at the end of the day
I have your love after all is said and done

Forever and always
I will be by your side
To comfort you
I am in love

How do I know and where do I start?
This feeling of well-being and happiness surrounds my heart
Every morning when I awake my dreams have come true as she is here in my arms
When together my senses are heightened by her setting them afire
Causing my heart to actually sing with the joy of being with her

Then when my day begins, time slows as I want to savour every moment with her
I try to retard my body clock so that there are not enough seconds in a minute,
minutes in an hour, hours in a day or days in a week
Yet time flies past even though I try to draw it out by savouring it, as I want to
be with her every second, every minute, every hour, every day and every week
through eternity
She has become my clock, my seconds, my minutes, my days and my weeks
Yes, I am in love.

Odean Scully

January

If I could return, to that yellow day
On our secret hillside, where the fairies play

If I could return, to our woodland den
With leave's glow for windows, Daylight shadows would bend

If I could return, where nymph dwell under'leaf
Cross our ivy'd bridge, Where I long to be

And do you remember
Where we would hide
When we'd play under moonlight
Your hand in mine

Yes I remember
As day turns to night
We'll sing under the moon
The fairies
You,
And I.

Sophie Revell

Heat Of The Night

You're on my mind and
In my heart
Beating next to mine
Kissing me all night
Till the break of dawn
Whispering in my ear
You love me
And you won't let me go
Until you hold me close
To your heart.

Amanda Jane Prince

Engagement

Would you be entwined . . . full of life . . .
If I were to strike you with a gold ring, honey?

Would you fall to my knees when I'm already on mine and say
Take me please

Would you be wicked and intent . . .
A life in imprisonment flatters from your lips

If there were a showering of gifts - or not,
That don't matter but I plot
'A happy-ever-after'

Do you think . . . or not?

Does he love me, or he loves me not

Either the ring will start to feel like a knot,
Killing off my love for circulation,
Either say yes or we're in the trash bin,
Ready to be recycled
. . . or it will let me in
To your heart, and we'd be one

You get on one knee and say
'Will you be the one . . . for me?'

And I say, 'Yes, certainly.'

Leanne Bridgewater

Lost Love

A hundred years ago or so
There would have been written proof
Of my love for you and yours for me.
Neatly written words with flamboyant loops
Wrapped around my hopes for the future.
Letters lovingly folded and refolded after
Being read and re-read for reassurance.
Carefully replaced in fragrant envelopes
Kept safe secure from the loveless world.
The years of our romance bound
In lavender ribbon securing our past together
And as time sped by and hopes faded
To be read, in an amber Autumn afternoon
Through watery blue eyes, for one last time.
So that I could re-live the love
Of a lifetime, not with regret
But with gratitude that once,
If only for a brief while,
I was truly loved by you.

But today all I have is vague memories
Of scattered telephone calls which
Once made are forever lost.
No mementos for old age, nor soft phrases
To prompt the failing memory,
Only the empty sound of a telephone
That no longer rings with
Love from you to me.

Sue Gerrard

Love Is Blind

They say
Love is blind
But if you're happy
With the girl you find

All that matters to you
Is you're content
With the love
You've been sent

We all need someone to love
That's our way
A partner
To help us through the day

At the end of the day
The battle won
If you can find
The right one

Frank Tonner

Untitled

A certain young man, determined to write a love poem to his fiancée,
Expressing how he felt toward her, came up with the following:

Sonnet

I'll love you, darling, till for evermore,
Oh, when you're near, you still this weeping heart,
With downy tones and mellow words of love,
You always seek my gladness to ensure,
I'd scale a mountain - sail the seven seas,
Cross jungles just to be alone with you,
I'll fight to stifle any forms of ire,
So you will each day keep conserved, your peace,
I love you madly - you must know that's true,
Since first I met you, life is far more whole,
If trouble knocks, it's straight to me you turn,
So I'll be there to make it right for you,
A million balls of light explode on cue,
As I lie, sipping champagne from your shoe.

Unfortunately, desiring to speak the words to his loved one,
And suffering the effects of an horrendous cold at the time,
This is what he actually said . . .

'Soddet!'

I'll love you Dalek, till forever bore,
Oh, wed your deer, you still this wee pig heart,
With dowdy toads add bellow words of love,
You always seek, by Gladys to Ed Shaw,
I'd scale a bowed Ted - sail the severed seas,
Cross juggles just to be a load with you,
I'll fight to stifle Eddie Forbes of Ire,
So you will each day, keep cod served, your piece,
I love you badly - you bust dough that's true,
Sid's first I bet you, life is far borehole,
If trouble docks, it's straight to be you turd,
So I'll be there to bake it right for you,
A billiard balls of light explode odd cue,
As I lie, sippig shab paid from your . . . *'Shoo!'*

They're no longer together!

Tony Reese

The Land Of Love

There is a wall across
      the land of love.
A high wall
      protected by guns.

The dirty Jordan runs between
      barbed wire fences
And the Sea of Galilee
      laps history.

We can carry on Abraham's unhappy choices
or let love live.

The bomb makers
have shared their atrocities
      across the world.
Fighting for freedom!

But love is the freedom we seek.
Forgiveness
      and turning the other cheek
the pathway
to the land of love.

Sommer B

Come And Be Beautiful

I see you on the picture
I can read your words
Need you here right now
Some joy in my world

It's been way too long
Since I saw you in the flesh
Make your way back
And we can start afresh

So much heartache around in this world
Happiness a rare gift to find
Dreams don't often come true anymore
Reality takes hold and bites

Right now in such a dark place
Convince me there is still light
Want to feel your soft touch on my face
Come to me lady tonight

Come and be Beautiful
Give me a love to believe
Come and be Beautiful
Be the making of me

Paul Holt

Valentine 2010

Two lonely persons, two shattered lives
  Nothing left, and nothing to do,
No hopes, no dreams, no will to live
  Trance-like, stumbling, drifting through.

At last, one day in June
  A phone call, out of the blue,
A meeting - two hearts awoke
  And found new love - 'twas me and you.

To live again and fall in love
  A deep, enduring passion, strong,
That salved away the lonely years
  The solitary exile having gone.

My husband, true, we've been through hell
  Life has dealt us a bitter blow,
To each other, we're still young
  Full of verve, get up and go.

Each year I write a few short lines
  To say how much I value you,
A love like ours transcends all time
  Wondrous, warm and shining through.

Elizabeth Stanley-Mallett

Forget-Me-Not

Snowdrops so pure, spring-like in winter's thaw,
Courageously blooming beneath the snow
That sparkles like jewels in the sun's rays,
And so love matures in the length'ning days.

Catananche's Cupid's dart marks the joy
Of a first love for a young girl and boy,
And in that first love with their arms entwined
They avow, 'I am yours if you are mine . . .'

As love mellows to the warm yellow tones
Of the marigold and orangy-bronze
Of the turning leaves in a gentle breeze,
They bathe in Love-in-a-mist azure seas.

When love falters and fades in October
Leaving Love-lies-bleeding red . . . tis over;
Amaranthus weeps o'er the young lovers,
Off'ring small comfort in autumn's cover.

Young love burns all too fast 'neath the hot sun
To cool swiftly under a hunter's moon.
Come the dawn's misty kiss 'pon the hilltop,
There blooms a small flower - Forget-me-not.

Gwendoline Douglas

From There To Eternity

When I was twelve you carried my books home from school
when I was fourteen you first declared your love for me
when I was sixteen you left me to work in foreign lands
when I was eighteen you found someone else and so did I
when I was nineteen we knew we were meant for each other.

Then we became us and our two separate lives became as one;
united against the world, always there to protect each other
from life's indiscriminate barbs and arrows. Our arms wrapped
around each other, even whilst apart. Constant, loving, supportive,
caring and always you were the one for me and I for you.

And now I reflect on thirty years passing, my eyes seeing that
young man and woman at the start of their unknown adventure,
their faces and hearts so eager for life's rich offerings. Did
those wishes, so keenly felt, when the years lay invitingly ahead
finally come true?

Not in a way that I could have seen with my naïve young eyes.
There's no sports car in the driveway, just a sensible one.
There's no large house, just a normal home with a mortgage.
There's no glorious career, just an ordinary day job.
There's no offshore bank account, just enough to keep us going.
Did we fail? I ask myself. No, because we have something so much
more precious.

An enduring, comforting, gentle love that sweeps aside all the
disappointments and difficulties that life leaves in its trail.
A shared history which can instantly recall the accumulation of
delights that have brought us joy over so many years.
Knowing that you are the most important person in someone's else's life.
Being with someone who laughs with you, supports you,
comforts you and makes you feel special.

Oh yes, we are truly rich.

Julie Hanks

Summer Stars Over The Sagrada Familia

Just occasionally I have broken free
from the terrible monotony of existence;
observing the sun escape from a crack
in dark, bruised, storm-filled clouds,
a spectacular flaming sunset,
sweet sound of melodious music or
the Sagrada Familia deep in love
with summer stars flickering high above.

I walk alone on a dank autumn evening,
shiver so pull up my collar
as a cruel wind races against my brow
yet contented that the streets are quiet.
I reach a pub where the lonely drink
feeling like Steppenwolf remembering
the Sagrada Familia deep in love
with summer stars flickering high above.

Guy Fletcher

Painting Cows

Poetry can heal the soul
likened to sweet music that once played
Like painting heals the heartache
The landscapes of my mind of memories left far behind.

Am I but a memory so seldom felt
That I sat beside the cows in summer and knelt
To paint the days, add a poem to pad
Never afraid to cry when I felt sad.
Do you cow, feel love like I do?
Let me paint a portrait of my outward view
Cast a long ago memory of a day like wildflower summer
Am I a memory so seldom felt,
pity my life for love that might have been.

Where lovers roam between heathers and cows
To wash away those wily hours
The palette, the paint, lies drying amidst the sunshine that streams
through the rainbow.
The night-time, where love lies dying amidst barren street lamp
The door like the verse unwritten.

Barry Powell

Love Poem II

You are my child
I loved you
You opened my eyes
To a New Day
You invited me in
To your world
So young
You are my child

You are my child
You brought me
Wonder
You brought me
Happiness
Your smile
Captivated my
Waiting heart
You are my child

You are my child
So brave
So daring
So adventurous
You had no fear
Survival is your name
You ran
You skipped
You persuaded
You delighted
You are my child

Margaret Bennett

Love Is

I miss you when you go
Wait the time for your return
That this time is somehow different
That's what love is
You consume my very being
Communicate that we are together
To others as well that we are joined
That's what love is
Light and sunshine come to mind
A smile that joy brings
A pleasure to see you and eye
That's what love is
Organisation and planning, features
Of the day that bringeth
Events and activities which blend us together
That's what love is
Shared meaning known only to a couple
Making closeness unspoken, apparent
Between us as two people over living time
That's what love is
Laughter is precious and well thought of
A chuckle at private humour, guarded and safe
Comfortable in that company that comes together
That's what love is
I still feel the stirring that comes from putting your hand in mine
Striding out jointly together
Speaking more loudly than words, we are as one
That's what love is
When we kiss it lingers on
Feels right, more than that
Soft lips meet mine, an age long passion
That's what love is
Come home loved one
The waited time is long enough
When coming through the door, you call out
That's what love is

Ron Constant

My Valentine

To Love You
Is a total gift
To be with you
Is what I wish

Through the good times
And the Bad
Together we will
Always stand

Hand in hand
We will stand tall
Together we will
Never fall

I Love You
And You Love Me
And that is how
It's meant to be

Catherine Uttley

Angel

I never believed in angels,
but now I do,
'twas your manifestation in another,
I sensed it was you;
for all those lonely nights I'd led,
walking such a desolate life . . .
it seemed all but dead,
now I want you for my wife.
My heart has been moved,
contemplations of your love,
if it's there, it's proved,
you bear something from above,
your drift into my thought,
your understanding of my suspension,
I was not bought,
by some fictitious invention.

Balm to my brow,
you've touched on the profound,
this is here and now,
today we are found,
but only by each other,
in a world of hate and distrust,
we've something to hold onto,
living's become more than a must,
and I'll stroll hand in hand,
with you in the sunset divine,
with a soul enlightened,
because I know you're mine.

Andrew Gruberski

Besotted By Thee . . .

Besotted by thee
By thine gazelle eyes upon my torched heart.
Thine softe, lovely lips, petals of a dew-stained rose,
givest me the supremest kiss, ne'er depart.

Thine winsome smile, like the hazel sky
of the autumn morning, ever-beauteous.
Thine resplendent laughter; like the eesome song
of the nightingale, resonating within, harmonious.

Thine sublime aura, like the rays of the dawned sun,
enchanting my senses thy ranunculus thing,
le belle ideal, an untarnished blossom.
daffodil of the earliest spring.

Thine charmed words, thy speaketh
forever; like the effulgent waterfall.
Thine scintillating aroma, mesmerised I behold
through the ages thy enthrall.

Thine thalassic hair, floweth like the
low sluiced seas, the world all agape.
Thine soporific deeds, with ardour, and
puissance, all malice a-swap.

Thine throbbing heart, beating alongside
mine; thine sweetest joy, thine wildest woe
shared with mine; never wane, my love;
for I am there for thee, ye gentle doe.

Thine dainty legs, graceful as the beating
ocean; rising and falling, dancing waves.
Thine immaculate emotions, like nature
herself, several octaves.

Thou of wholeness impersonified,
pulchritude dimensioned, a new Adonis.
My benefactor, my life's blood,
thy sustain me from a dark abyss.

Thou of radiance of nature's zenith,
beauty born from whispering sound.
Thou art the cherry-cheeked maiden,
hast the world stand astound.

Thou art the godsent cherub;
to love thee is a glimpse of Heaven.
Thou hast the fatal gift of beauty;
bewitching a pantheon of brethren.

Thou art the exquisite lea,
infinite, far-reaching shine.
Thou has the golden touch, withered leaf
come alive, thou art mine.

Thou art me, hast me enraptured,
love triumphed, bereft of movement.
Defeated to thine beautiful strains,
I art servant to thee, thy ambient.

Conquer me, daughter of Mars;
Thine happiness is glory to me.
Thine loving light illuminating
every world, not one, two, but three.

Beau, o dearest one, come to my arms.
Thine uxorious embrace is an oasis.
Punish me, let my villainy suffer,
but takest not my loving basis.

Mon amour, eftsoons the world revolves,
as the cycle of time sweeps us away,
I remain clinging to thee, o angel,
love no decay.

Yet, here I lie spurned,
Blood on the rock.
All around, the enigmatic waters
of Neptune's brine, mock.

Dost thee love me?
Hast thee feelings of coquettish?
Art thee oblivious to my advances?
Art mine amoroso gone skittish?

For how dost I lovest thee?
Till the ends the soul can reach, passion rife.
With every breath, smile and tear,
loving thee with all my life.

Abhishek Ravichandran (16)

Girlfriend

Girlfriend's always got my back and always by my side
Encouraging, supporting me through times both good and bad.
The bus won't come, the car broke down - Girlfriend is my ride.
In testing times be sure, for me, she'd give up all she had.

Girlfriend is the only one who understands my plight.
When my man hasn't come home and he finds it hard to talk.
When every time we try it turns into a nasty fight,
Girlfriend is the one with me each time he takes a walk.

Girlfriend will drop everything to help me when I'm sad.
She'll make me laugh when all I really would have done is cry.
She'll be the one to calm me down when life has made me mad
And never let me give up anything worth one last try.

Girlfriend, in her special way will tell it to me straight
And warn me he's no good for me, there's better in this world.
Advising me to leave him before love turns into hate.
For here I'm torn apart while he is out with other girls.

Girlfriend buys me chocolate when I'm stuck with PMT
And turn into a monster from whom everyone will run.
Whatever form of trouble, she's the one who'll rescue me
And coax me gently outwards when I hide from everyone.

Girlfriend was the one who always got me back on track.
A special individual who always held my trust.
I didn't see it coming when she knifed me in the back
And watched our friendship fade away and crumble into dust.

Girlfriend tried to be the 'other woman' in his life.
Ensuring we stayed fighting, making sure we stayed apart.
How funny - after all her work, he's making me his wife.
For under all the pain there was true feeling in our hearts.

Girlfriend never told me why she cheated, schemed and lied,
But said a little part of her wanted to be like me.
The friend I had looked up to, whom I'd claimed with so much pride,
Was bilious and twisted and consumed by jealousy.

Girlfriend's not my girlfriend now, I've many other friends.
But still I miss her deeply and I mourn what used to be.
I understand life's cycles now - new starts, pain when things end.
I wish her well. My life goes on - in peace and happily.

Natasha Jules

Love From Your Valentine

His note, 'Love from your Valentine',
Handed to his jailer's daughter
Was the last caring act in time
In two hundred and sixty-nine
Of a martyr bound for slaughter
For holding marriage was no crime.

The fourteenth of February
Named Saint Valentine's Day
Became his anniversary
When shy young lovers, hearts afire,
In a secretive sort of way
Write notes to one they most desire.

Although teasing fun may have gone
From the games stable couples play.
Like us, their love's been built upon
Nothing mean, rude, crude or passé
But on faith that won't fade away
And prove of worth on Judgement Day!

So my delightful Valentine
You hold me in your beauty's trance
And bind me with your radiance
Which no other soul will outshine
Yet keeps me safe with love's lifeline
And make each day one long romance.

Ronald Rodger Caseby

My True Love, The Mistress Of My Heart

I first saw her when I was but a child.
And although much older than me, I fell truly, madly, deeply and
passionately in love at first sight, to be forever her slave from the moment
we first touched. As I've grown older, my love and passion for her only
increased with each beat of my heart. Captivating it and my soul forever.
She has the heart and soul of an angel, so peaceful and serene, bringing
such a sense of elation, almost ecstasy, to be in her company. Yet so full of
life and anger that she can destroy anyone and anything in her path,
if she so wishes. So please, don't dare to try her patience.
She has the warmth of beauty of a summer's day. Basking you in her
comforting embrace and bringing life to all she comes into contact with.
Yet can be so cold as to freeze the life right out of you. Leaving you frozen
as solid as a statue in a museum for all to gaze upon.
She has the beauty, grace and elegance of a prima ballerina. Taking delicate,
precise steps across the stage of life whilst performing her art. Yet, when
angered and tormented. She will come charging like a runaway freight train
crashing into the terminus, spreading chaos, carnage and death all around her.
Some love her, yet others hate her. Some fear her, yet others attempt to take
liberties with her. Heed these simple words of wisdom, because all must respect
her! Those who don't, inevitably pay the ultimate price with their life.

All too many, never to be seen again.
Here I am in my second half of my life and find I cannot be without her.
Every day I need her more and more, to worship, adore and touch her.
To feel her touch upon my skin, her all-embracing caress. Being with and
around her is like a drug surging through my veins. Carrying with it, a
sensation of life, living, joy, comfort and bliss throughout my entire being.
Be it a day where she is warm or cold, peaceful and serene, or angry and
just waiting to explode. I need her as much as I need the air that I breathe.
For without her, the breathing is but an exercise in endless futility,
frustration, heartache and sorrow.

When that fateful day or night finally arrives, where I have drawn my last breath. Then I beg of you, grant me this one request. Wrap me in canvas and bind me with heavy chains. Take me out to her and lower me into her belly, so that I might at last truly join her and become a part of her very being. My soul spending the rest of eternity with her. The bringer of all life to our planet. My true love, the mistress of my heart, the deep, blue, endless sea.

Andy - Scrawl of the Wild Ones

Full Circle

The open wounds from being torn apart,
Lays a broken heart,
Bewildered, the loss,
Tears of sadness, the cost.

Searching, wanting to be found,
Cries silently not to make a sound,
Time is a healer,
No matter who's the dealer.

Heartache begins to make amends,
With the help of a true friend,
Happiness is found,
Full circle comes around.

To be cared,
Love is shared,
When seeing that special smile,
Makes everything worthwhile.

Jo Benson

My Mother Is . . .

The most amazing woman,
That I will ever know.
A loving, caring person,
With a kind and warming soul
She reminds me of a mountain,
Very strong and standing tall
She helps us through the troubled times,
She's a credit to us all.
She is someone I am proud of,
And a person that I admire
I'm just lucky that I have someone,
As special as my Mother

Barbara C Perkins

There May Be . . .

There may be a plan to unite
Every maid with a special man.
But remorseless fate may close love's gate.
Somehow perhaps reordained that
Spinsters and bachelors often remained
To a sad past inescapably chained.
Who can read the runes or comprehend
A heart's sombre tunes, leaving love in ruins?
Yet, it may not be the end and
A kindly heaven will offend,
And to a desperate prayer a friendly ear lend.
Dying embers of a lonely passion may be still able to
Glow, o once more eternal love can grow.
Burning with furnace heat, the
New challenges of Cupid meet.

Graham Watkins

In A Mood

When your partner's in a huff,
The going can get very rough,
Nothing is ever good enough.

If he's in the blackest mood,
He can be so terribly rude,
What happened to the man who wooed?

He criticises and has to moan,
He likes for me to hear him groan,
No respect for me he has shown.

His charm has left him way behind,
The man who once was very kind,
Now everything's to him a bind.

He will not go out for a walk,
He's silent, does not want to talk,
He's changed from cheese into chalk.

He bangs around, he slams the door,
He mutters, swears and stamps the floor,
Don't know if I can take much more

What have I done to make him so
Irritable, nasty, feeling low?
Cannot guess - it must be bad though.

He drives off in his car so fast.
Tyres screeching, he goes flying past
The neighbours, leaving me in peace at last.

June Melbourn

Minus You

No more laundry to hang out and no more plants to pot.
A waste of a daily newspaper; a song sang that you will never hear.
Nothing is tidy. Everything is lost. All it needed was the last of your
woman's touch.
A precious gesture that lasted a second is as vivid to me as yesterday.
The clothes you lived in and the spectacles you wore to read
are as useless now as your toothbrush by the sink
and the worn out flannel you cleansed your living body with.
Radio 4 lost a listener, the local farm shop lost a customer
and I lost much of me.
All of a sudden I have no direction in a world
which doesn't seem able to rest.
Are you at rest? Can I rest with you?
People walk faster than me and they walk as though
they are going somewhere much more important than I ever am, or ever was.
You were my guardian; we always walked at our own pace,
steady and together.
I am learning on my own now
And I am doing well by myself; following your prints.
People will ask where you are and I still can't answer them.
In years to come I hope to accept that you are gone
But when I need to reach you, I still can, can't I?

Sophie Phelps

Untitled

Joy and happiness
Will come your way,
Wait patiently.
Depend on yourself,
No one else.
Then one day you may find love in someone
Else's hand.
Happy, carefree, love and honesty
You will find some hope for your
New coming life,
That may surely be.
A love everlasting
Will be yours
For all eternity.

Deborah Storey

The Pain Of Love

The pain of love can be bad,
Sometimes it can be very sad
It can hurt and rip you inside
It can make you want to run away and hide
Then, your friend says to you
You will fine, just give it a little time
You are right, it stabs like a knife
No one can take the hurt away
It's on your mind all the time
And it stabs like a knife
You see him, or her
And you feel twisted inside
And it stabs like a knife
Then, one day the hurt will go away
You will wonder, whatever happened to the one
That made you feel like
You got stabbed by a knife.

Pamela Lutwyche

Hearts And Bones

One and one half wandering angels
Walking from his door to her door
Upon damp, dark pavements
They won't be ignored
With prior engagements removed for the night.
Nobody said the ending would be their reward,
The arcs of a love affair
They won't be restored.
The words and music took their bodies
And placed them into one
Their hearts and their bones
They won't come undone.

Siegfried Baber

Photo Scenthesis

Photos placed beside the bed,
Memories of a novel read,
Freudian dreams so deep and rare,
Now confined to immortal care,
Pulses raced and linen stained,
Body fluids and emotions drained,
That Special Scent torments the mind,
Where past and present and future bind,
Fleeting sightings of Eden's trinity,
Of Love and Hope and Merged infinity,
DNA confirms the perfection.
Of soulmates spawned,
Through Angelic connection,
Romantic holidays in Heaven and Hell,
The Human nut has left its shell,
How many lives must we go through,
Before we become immune to the
Existence Flu?

Edward J Daly

The Pain Of Loss

(Inspired by Una, a very brave lady)

When your heart has just broken and your spirits are low,
encouraging teardrops that so easily flow

When you don't understand and you can't comprehend,
the disintegration of a life so profound

Perturbed by the days and isolation of night,
grabbing hold of each image and hanging on tight

Savouring memories sometimes you are cross,
the photos, the laughter, the feelings of loss

Just another long day when the haze will not clear,
when you feel you have lost everything that is dear

Restlessly tossing and turning at night,
not closing your eyes in case you lose sight

Of the memories so treasured, so real and so warm,
afraid of the demons that in your head swarm

As into oblivion you gently will slide,
a tear-stained pillow will your sorrow hide

You will sleep, you will wake, you will come to accept,
all the things now so painful that leave you bereft

Remember and listen, and cradle that voice
then move slowly forward, you do have a choice

Jackie Davies

True Love

'Weeping and gnashing of teeth'
'Outer darkness'
'Utterly consumed with terrors'
'Everlasting fire'
'Everlasting punishment'
'I am tormented in this flame'
'How can we escape the damnation of Hell?'

God is not willing that any should perish,
Oh how He longs to make us His own.
Oh how He yearns to freely forgive us,
That we might be His - and His alone.
    When life on this Earth comes to an end -
    Where will I be?
    Heaven above? Hell beneath?
    Where will I spend eternity?

When Christ the spotless Son of God
Died at Calvary,
He bore the punishment we deserve -
He died to set us free.

He wants to free us from our sin
That leads to death and Hell.
He wants to give new life within -
A home in Heaven as well.

We have a choice as to how we live.
We can follow our own desires,
Or we can come to God through Christ
To flee everlasting fire.

We have offended a Holy God
With wickedness and sin;
Only Christ can cleanse the heart
And give true peace within.

For God so loved the world He gave
His only begotten Son;
That whosoever believeth in Him
Everlasting Hell would shun.

His soul would live with God on high
In that sublime abode,
Far exceeding all we've known -
When freed from sin's great load.

God is not willing that any should perish.
He has paved the way,
That we might escape the terrors of Hell
And dwell in eternal day.
When life on this Earth comes to an end -
Where will I be?
Heaven above? Hell beneath?
Where will I spend eternity?

Marion Tinkler

A Swirl Of Leaves

A swirl of leaves made you laugh, and your lips, prone
To linger - sought mine; so in love, we were as one
That autumn day; I couldn't know you'd be taken away
And I would be left all alone.

You scooped me up in your arms so strong . . .
I felt our love would last forever and anon
Then as we made impassioned vows, we two . . .
Another gust whipped up a swirl of leaves.

It is autumn again - I text you on a mobile phone
But a door is slammed in my face; you have found someone
else, and ignore my anguished plea, to see you.
I go my solitary way once more, for you are gone
It seems, like . . . a swirl of leaves.

Delphine

Love's Lament

(As a person who has Alzheimer's the thoughts of Love and Loss are constantly on my mind which made me write this poem about my dear wife and my inner feelings)

My head lay cushioned upon your silken breast,
your tears of sorrow caressing at my nape,
as the fingers of an angel soothing my brow,
yet the heart within you was echoing out lament,

For those destined moments since set to one side
as the confusions within me will not subside
this illness of my mind is just tearing me apart,
but this loving kiss, I can still place on your heart,

I'd dreamed of twilight years walking hand in hand,
the romance of our love defying the blossoms of time,
for the love within your heart had been more than mere words,
since you entered my life with the tenderness of your soul,

Now as my being diminishes betwixt life and death,
yet still comely unto my eyes is your every breath,
so weep not a tear for what you behold in your arms,
as my spirit will guide thee, ever steadfast and strong.

Then whence I lay my head upon the soft clouds of God,
embalm my body with every essence of your love,
thus as your guardian angel I shall forever oversee,
until time doth come, for ye to accompany me,

Thence once more we shall enfold our undying love,
never parting us again with sorrowful lament . . .

Barry Pankhurst

Yet . . .

I lie in the essence of him,
My head rests on the pillow where his head lay,
A love that never will be mine,
Yet . . .

I watched him shake away sleep,
And my body ached to be there with him,
In that bed by his side
Him and I
Entwined as lovers should entwine,
Yet . . .

He talks, and I listen
To this man whose love I can never hold,
Love which flows through my stretched veins,
I want to reach out and take him
Ignite a spark within him,
Yet . . .

Now committed to some dusty corner within his brain
I suppress my thoughts for him,
My feelings for him,
They lie dormant, sleeping,
Will they ever awaken again?

Unsure thoughts of him tread softly.

Yet . . .

Mark Marsh

Your Love Is Right

My Valentine, dream tonight
So much love
So much care
Every night
You are there
With me you will stay
Every day
Your long blonde hair
Blows in the air
So much style
So much flair
Your kisses
Are so divine
A love so fine
A dream of love
All the time
Now you are mine.

Gordon Forbes

We Are One

I sit and wait
In anticipation
Of our meeting
I hear your footsteps
Approaching you sit
Down next to me and
Our eyes lock
we look at each other
My heart melts
Your hand gently
Enfolds mine
Once more we are one.

Penelope Ann Kirby

Retirement

Love is in an easy chair
Just to see you sitting there
A quiet room at peace and still
memories linger on their photo frame, they may have left
But it's love and peace that still remains
I see our children still at play
As if it was only yesterday
The fire reflecting on your face
You look up and smile
And I can see that your eyes are saying that you still love me
Time has flown and years have passed
Home with you is all I ask
I don't need to travel to Paris or Rome
For my life is you with me
Here at home.

Trevor Mercer

Ruby Wedding

We married when we were quite young
Our love was true, our bond so strong
Our children brought us so much pleasure
Such happy days we both will treasure

They now have families of their own
They visit and they often phone
Forty years have just flown past
Still our devotion holds us fast.

You're still my husband and my friend
I will be yours until life's end
My journey as a wife and mother
I wouldn't swap for any other.

Rhona Bayliss

The Corruption Of Love

you can fight all you want
but you've already broken my will
I stand with nothing left
nothing left for you to kill

you came into my world
and left a trail of destruction
all that was good
you turned with your corruption

you fought with hate
and we fought with love
but you're standing tall
so it just wasn't enough

so now that all is done
tell me what I've learned?
was your lesson taught?
in the fires that you burned?

Mervin RJ Taylor

Love From Above

First a dream, then a shout
as I turn over and reach out
I look at your pillow, then I stare
Then I realise you're not there.
Tears and heartache, I feel the pain
why you passed away, I can't explain
Being your wife, I will always treasure
my love for you, is my life's pleasure
you were loving, faithful, forever true
my wonderful husband, that was you.

Patricia Dibble

Wanted A Man

I need a man in my bed
Not any Tom, Dick, Harry or Fred
Someone to hold
When the nights are cold
Someone good-looking and strong
Someone to give me a cuddle
When my day has been in a muddle
Will he ever come along?
Someone to feel close
Next to me
That would certainly be
Love-ly
Someone nice to keep me warm
Something different from the norm
I would then feel content
And give a little giggle of merriment.

Caroline Janney

Skin Of A Lover

Skin draws wanted affection
Opens up senses, feelings in mind
Things like sex satisfaction
Legs intertwined
Skin reacts like a magnet
The rubbing sensation is fine
When the mouth touches mouth
And the tongues intertwine
Skin interlocked fingers
Arms wrapped round each other
Love senses run wild
With the skin of a lover.

John Hickman

Lost Love

Now I once knew a sweet nurse who
Came from the Emerald Isle.
She had gleaming teeth that shone beneath
Her lovely dazzling smile.
'Twas no wonder why she caught my eye
That morning long ago.
From where she came, what was her name?
I simply had to know.

As she came in that day, to the ward where I lay
I was instantly struck by her charm.
I watched so intent, as to each bed she went
As I lay with my head on my arm.
When she reached me at last, I had to talk fast,
In order to learn all I could.
I was left in no doubt that I must ask her out,
For all that she told me, was good.

We conversed every day of my very short stay,
And my feelings for her grew and grew
How I longed to embrace her sweet angel face,
And by now I was certain she knew.
So on the day of my leave I took hold of her sleeve
Telling her all that I wished to say
As I held her so near, I said, 'I love you my dear,
And I can't bear to leave you today.'

'Oh, I'd love you,' said she, 'to come down and see me
For I too, know that you I will miss.'
I was over the moon to have won her so soon,
And our lips met again with a kiss.
There were tears in my eye, as I wished her goodbye,
I felt one, run down on my cheek,
'I'll come down on the train, to see you again,
On Monday or Tuesday, next week.'

So in sunshine or snow down to Bath I did go
To see that Colleen, so sweet
With her by my side and my heart full of pride
She really swept me off my feet.
Then she went away, for a month's holiday,
Where, she told me, she met an old friend.
He then bought her a ring, they planned to wed in the spring
But for me I'm afraid, 'twas the end.

Kenneth Ody

You Are A Lovely Bird

Once I see a robin my dear
It makes me think of you
Perky, chirpy, cheery, revered
Spread warmth in all you do
Captivate with cute neatness
Of bold spirit and great pride
Deem an eye treat at its best
Hoped will always longer bide
Your magic glow spells Christmas
Copy such smartness only could a few
Can write books of your praises lass
Now just too long overdue
Sweetest bird to all so clear
A forever welcome and dear friend
Well looked out for throughout the year
My best wishes to you now send
You are a lovely bird.

Thomas McConnachie

I Would Always Think Of You

You are my sunshine,
You're so beautiful and nice;
Soft, like a summer breeze in my face,
Bubbly, like a mountain stream, cool like ice.
When you come to see me it's like paradise.

When you smile
You make my whole life worthwhile;
Your lips are sweet like wine,
I want to hold you all the time.
Your warm and tender touch makes me long to be with you so much.

When your eyes sparkle and shine,
They seem to tell me you are mine.
Your birthday cake will have another candle,
of which there is no doubt,
Sorry I can't spare the breath to help you blow them out.

You lighten and brighten every day,
Ever since you came my way;
With you in my life I'm never blue,
You make me happy when I'm with you.

I love you and you say you love me too,
Life is so sweet just loving you;
You are the one who makes my sun shine bright,
I think about you day and night.

I love you and all your charms,
I love you most when you're in my arms;
Everything's fine, everything's alright,
Just can't wait to see you on your birthday night.

Many happy days we share are quite alright,
I cherish the moments I hold you tight;
I love you with all my heart
And always will with sheer delight.

A Tapestry Of Thoughts

You're always there to comfort me,
When I'm sad or blue;
And if we are ever to part,
You will still be here within my heart.

I love to hear you when you sing,
Wish I could write you a song;
I hope this poem cheers you up,
From your ever loving pup.

I hope you will carry on
And always be who you really are;
To me you are like my guiding star.

This is just a poem to let you know,
Just how much I love you so;
And how much you mean to me,
I love you so specially.

I keep wondering it's so strange,
Love is strange, I just can't change;
But when my life on Earth is done,
I hope you remember all the fun.

Even if I met someone new, I would always think of you.

John Walker

Love At First Sight

(For Louise)

A child at the time in a pretty summer frock
She was dragged along to pre-season
With Dad and the chaps, whilst Mum chose to stay indoors, why?
To check on the new signings.
Going through the motions in a friendly,
To see what chance, if any
The team had for a bit of success that coming season.

Thousands of fans and their families
Were scattered about warm concrete terracing
On a balmy London Saturday afternoon
Like Dad and the chaps wearing sunglasses
Casting knowing critical eyes over newly assembled talent
To see if it was deemed worthy of wearing a club shirt.

Playing and dancing up and down seemingly endless steps
Behind the goal, with other contented young kids as free as a bird
Dad escorted her to the Ladies
(Lord knows how many blooming times)
Waited outside for her, and when they came back
The chaps gave her Polo mints, and taught her wonderful songs
That everyone joined in with,
Laughing and clapping loudly after each one.

When singing and the game was over
Dad's best mate held her hand
As they talked excitedly, mingling with the crowd
Walking up the steep steps toward a bright blue sky
At the top of the terracing they turned around
To look down onto the pitch sparkling like a jewel in the evening sun.

It was love at first sight
She's had an ongoing affair of the heart with our club ever since
Her knowledge of team matters has no bounds
Her loyalty has cost me a small fortune

Now she supports herself and our club I'm amazed
That which once was a small young child in a pretty summer frock
Way back then has blossomed into womanhood
Mastered a quite enviable vocabulary of words
Any of which can be used to describe loudly and in quite infinite detail
The failings of the common . . . footballer!

Kevin Raymond

The Vampire's Kiss

He moves closer
Lips parted, he teases, no kiss
Just his breath caressing my face.
For a moment I can't think straight
I'm dying inside - agony and
Ecstasy rocking me to the core.

He turns his head, slightly to one side;
My breast rising and falling in anticipation.
His lips brush mine for less than a second;
Eyes tinted with obsession.
A stray lock of hair falls loose
Over his forehead
(I don't want to brush it back into place.)

His mouth gently exploring mine,
A slight pang turns into a raging hunger;
As kisses move from lips to neck to shoulder.
And then and then and . . .
My blood now flowing through his veins.

Vicky Stevens

Getting There?

I can look at the sea again . . .
Almost . . .
Without even thinking of you,
But then those waves come crashing in
With hues of jade, grey-blue.

A decade, and focus is hazy
Of my crazy soul drawn straight to you,
Then that wavy line drawn
Under our affair
Diffuses in aquamarine-blue.

I can look at the sea once more
Only
When my mind can re-focus anew
And its passion for waves
Reminds me no more
Of waves of lost passion. And you.

Maybe if I ghost the coast
Quietly,
On some moonlight-free inky-black night,
Your eyes - cool grey-blue -
Will haunt me no more
With their luminous ocean-deep light.

Nadia Nuth

How Much?

How much do you love me?
You often ask of me
How many little fishes
Are swimming in the sea?
Will you be true to me?
Is another plea
How many hours of daylight
Can there ever be?
Do you love me sincerely?
Another question for me
You ought to know by now
To take me seriously
Will you love me later
When I'm growing old?
If we live that long
Our story will unfold
We'll grow old together
Happy now and forever
Like two turtle doves
Cooing in a tree
Always together
Just you - and me.

Martin Selwood

A Very Special Love

It was a very special love.
A love of the mind, heart and soul.
It came about one bitter winter's night
when just the act of exhaling one's breath
crystallised around the midnight air.

I saw you emerge from the undergrowth.
You stood very still, facing me, hesitant and unsure.
Your eyes were angry and I sensed and saw their intensity
yet I was unafraid.

Your coat, so thin and still wet from yesterday's snow
had soaked through to your skin.
So I hurriedly heated some milk with a drop of brandy and you
drank it all like a dying man - now suddenly reprieved!

I took you in and gave you shelter and food.
Slowly, very slowly, you became my friend and I yours.
You began to demonstrate a deep, profound intellect
and your cleverness amazed not only myself, but others.
As like, a tired, aged, old and abused shrub
you blossomed like a newly opened flower
that had been rejuvenated by a hand that nurtured and cared.

Slowly, after time had slipped and slithered
down the months and years
we had wormed and wriggled our way into each other's hearts
so deeply, that our love for each other
became one of besotted adoration.

Our years together were peaceful, happy and free
although short - too short!
Cancer deprived you of your happy life
and myself of a much loved companion and friend.
I will not forget your brave stoicism and the love you
constantly gave and showed me.

I put fresh flowers on your grave today and talked to you
of our wonderful times - our long walks with the sun and shadows
seeping down across the fields
and friends we would meet along the way.
You touched many lives, the impact of your personality,
strong and deep.
We will not forget your gentleness and sense of fun
when playing pranks or hide-and-seek.
All these things I remember and visualise in my mind's eye,
but now I am bereft and lost in a downward spiral of grief
that will continue on, as will the love we shared.

You are gone, and I am left with a silence,
where hope was!
Goodbye, my dear friend and beloved feline.

Alexandra Law-Hazel

Love's Exit

'If love is a clown with a shiny red nose,
When the greasepaint's removed, does daylight expose,
A juggling new game-play in a shiny red suit?'
And so the red-painted smiles on the woman's face have now gone,
Just clay-like grey lines show that pain lingers on.
The dressing room is bare, just the wig on the stand,
The make-up in boxes and clothes that have gone.
A concert now ended, it's been a long tale,
This woman, now old, rests on the rail!
An audience who once applauded have gone to stage right,
Not just for today, but for the long night
So if love is a clown with a shiny red nose
When the daylight exposes it silently goes!

Christine Flowers

Silent Film

Would you sit there laughing
At a man unclean for days,
Who can't feel that he's starving
But is slimmer than a fray?
A curled up mess upon the floor,
With sick stains on his shirt.
Girls' names fade to 'W*****'
As empty bottles blurt.
This broken boy is one of us,
And though all things repeat,
Words so used won't mean enough,
But stories cannot speak.
TV hearts we see will sing,
Oh! isn't love a funny thing?

Steven Wraight

My Darling Malcolm

If you were here with me today
I would see a glimmer of hope
because since the day that you left
I haven't been able to cope,
why you left I will never know,
you hurt me so much
much more than you could ever know,
the day that you walked out of the door
my world fell apart,
because I loved you so much
right from the very start,
if you appeared in my life again today
My darling Malcolm
I wouldn't send you away.

Linda Casey

My Wife

She is now so slow and ungainly, but love is in my heart,
I hate to see her struggling, and I never want to part,
The memories of our younger days, the laughter and the tears,
She used to chase me round the house, I'm rolling back the years,
The meals she made are not forgotten,
But now they have become the past
I'll love her until the end of time, my memories will always last,
She may be struggling because of aches and pains
Which have gained a hold on her today,
There are those who say that if not used, then muscles face decay,
No matter how she struggles using her walking frame.
I've not been very patient with her, but nothing will I gain,
But love is deep within me, it will always remain in my heart,
Until the very last moment, when one of us must depart.
Our memories are of happier times.
Are in an album of good times shared.
But I hate to see her struggling, but she still knows I've cared.
I don't want to see her go into hospital, because I'll be on my own.
Although I could still visit her or seek some information,
By using the telephone.
Our love has grown ever stronger, my feelings for her will never depart
When God planted the seed of love for her fondly in my heart.

James Ayrey

Cinquain

Some men,
Chase girls for fun
At work, and play, they stray.
True lovers are content with one.
Pure love.

A R David Lewis

Apologetics Not Apologies

Please do not mistake my role today,
The goal at stake is your life,
Please listen carefully to all that I say.
Because above your heads hangs a knife.

Apologists are not here to make an excuse,
To flimflam, fudge or to conceal.
My arguments are aimed to set you loose,
And God's loving plan to reveal.

'The church is hypocritical' some will say,
And 'Why does God let bad things go on?'
'You support slavery, you hate the Gay'
Before you can answer, they're gone.

But the apologist will gladly sit down,
And answer all of your false fears,
He will dry your tears; wipe away your frown,
And explain how God's plan is clear.

The things that you have heard are not true,
But the lies spread by the enemies' tongue,
They confuse and divide and hoodwink you,
To keep you from where you belong.

So go right ahead, and ask us to explain,
But please then to give us a chance,
To open God's word, and make all things plain,
Don't make up your mind in advance.

I tell you the truth, you sons of men
Our Gospel is of forgiveness and love,
Yes, only the Father knows the where and the when,
But the rest is given to us from above.

Bill Hayles

Love

Love can be a butterfly
Dancing in the sun,
But when the skies turn grey
And storms begin to blow
Then butterflies are gone.

Love can be a candle light
Flickering in the dark,
But when chilly draughts begin to blow
Or the candle melts away
The flame becomes a spark.

Love should be eternal,
An all-consuming fire of giving,
Not desire;
So when the storms of life pass by
Or shadows close about
Its warmth will give protection
Its light will be a guide,
And even when its giver's gone
Love shines on.

Allan Lewis

Cry A River

If I cry a river,
Will you sail on home to me?
See the light that flickers
At the window of my heart.
It flames like a beacon to our love.
Guiding, beckoning, caressing.

Clare Todd

Pearl Anniversary

Words are used in poems to convey our feelings and thoughts,
Whether it be sadness or joy, but love is a word that cannot
be explained.
Some would say it is
a great feeling of jubilation
and warmth, that comes from
deep within our hearts.
Today we celebrate our Pearl Anniversary.
When I stood at the altar and looked into
your eyes I knew then, that the flame
I carried for you deep within my heart,
would always burn brightly for you.
If our souls were like mirrors
you would see that our love
for each other is written in
the stars.
Those vows of love that I
made then, still stand true
today.

Brian Ross

Love Is An Oxymoron

Love is an oxymoron,
It is such an exquisite pain,
It is such a wonderful disaster,
And such an easily fathomable enigma,
And such a straightforward conundrum.

Mick Nash

A Plea To Saint Valentine

Dear Saint Valentine, this day of yours
Seems to have been made for blushing youth,
For those who stand tiptoe on the brink of life,
Still firm and beautiful. But what, we ask,
About the woman whose children have flown the nest?
Loves the world, still feels young, but sidelined,
Like an invisible wallflower at a cosmic party,
Petals fading, but dying to be asked to dance?
You will see us, if you really look, hovering around
The stands of roses, looking down at their faces,
Their velvet ephemeral faces, their glorious deep reds,
Wondering if we should buy our own, relegated
As we are to housekeepers, to rememberers of birthdays,
To food stockers and menu makers. I pause with a woman,
An unknown woman with a pleasant face, and we smile.
And she says, with a catch in her voice, that she is planning
To buy roses for the grave of her son now in Heaven.
And my eyes gleam tears for her. I murmur in sympathy.
My loneliness suddenly trivial. So dear Saint Val,
Blessed saint, find us all a dream love with the biceps of Raffa,
The lips and sulky presence of Brad or Jude, the charm of George,
A heavenly voice like Josh to serenade us on a sea-swept beach.
And above all the humour to make us laugh out loud.
We will awake on the morrow to find that we are still alive
With passion, rumpled and flushed, strewn with petals.
Rubenesquely dimpled and sprawled, rosily wreathed in smiles
And with a long-lost feeling of having been truly loved.

Liz Davies

Real Love

Chinese New Year and Valentine
In 2010 were on the same day
While these two festivals have very different origins
There are some similarities that go their way
In both cases loved ones give gifts
To express their love for one another
Whether roses on Valentine or red packets of money
They represent tokens of love to uncover
Jesus told his disciples to love one another
Because through them people would see
The great love God has for us
Shown in them for you and for me
It's a different love from the romantic couples
And the love between friends and kin
It is an unselfish love displayed by Jesus
When He went to the Cross for our sin

Catherine M Armstrong

Emotional As Charged

We are emotional people, you and I,
But we are not alone, my Wonderful Friend.
Christ visiting Lazarus was seen to cry.
Of deep abiding Love there can be no end,
Will the Fountains of Unction ever fail?
Try telling a dog not to wag its tail!

Tony Sainsbury

Mary's Prayer : A Weeping Heart

In prayer dear God this Christmas time
Keep safe in thine arms my son (Mark)
Forgive this weeping heart of mine
That mourns his passing on.

In prayer sweet Jesus this Christmas time
Forgive my weeping heart
For being so sad this birthday thine
Bereft of festive thoughts.

In prayer kind friends this Christmas time
Let not this verse deter
Forgive this weeping heart of mine
Each day throughout each year.

In prayer my son this Christmas time
For whom these tears are for
Mine heart shall weep forever for thine
Till come we meet once more.

Peter Terence Ridgway

My Love Of My Life

I love waking up next to you,
It's like arousing from a dream,
My first woken breath,
I inhale your face, I see,
You laying next to me,
With a smile upon your face,
So handsome, so wonderful,
A delectable taste,
A taste of your lips,
Your arms around me,
Satisfying my appetite,
My stomach not rumbling,
I'm content, I am happy,
For I'm on cloud nine,
Even when it rains,
You make my sun shine,
I feel safe, taken care of,
You're a real rare breed,
Loved by his friends,
For the whole world to see,
What a great catch I have,
I'm not letting you go,
You're my partner in crime,
I need you for the show,
The show of my life,
And you have got the leading part,
You have the permission,
To keep hold of my heart.

Emma McNamara

Tying The Knot

'I feel quite faint,' the bridegroom sighed.
'Hush . . . here she comes - here comes the bride,'
The best man murmured, trying to sound calm,
As the vision in white on her father's arm
Swished down the aisle with the grace of a swan,
With two cute little bridesmaids following on.

The groom turned around to admire his bride;
With a couple more steps she was there at his side.
And, as the assembly of guests fell mute,
He made one last endeavour to straighten his suit,
And wished that he hadn't drunk that double gin
Before leaving home, as it hadn't helped him.

The time had arrived for the service to start
And the bride vowed to love him with all of her heart,
While he promised faithfully never to stray,
And she'd gladly cherish, honour . . . and obey.
As the pair, now wed, strolled back up the aisle,
Their nervousness waned and they started to smile,

Enjoying the moment, in love and elated.
The sun shone outside; the photographer waited.
And, with the formalities all taken care of,
The only thing now that they had to beware of
Was the content of the best man's oration:
A prospect to fear after too much libation!

They needn't have worried for, as it transpired,
The best man stayed sober: a feat they admired.
And everyone said they'd had a great time -
The food was fantastic, and so was the wine.
Then it was time to bid them farewell,
So they said their goodbyes and left the hotel.

On the way to the airport they stole many kisses,
So madly in love were this man and his missus.
And, once on the plane, which was bound for Mauritius,
They ate passion fruit, which they found quite delicious;
And toasted their future as man and wife,
Together, for now . . . and the rest of their lives.

Heather Pickering

The Android's Burial

'Twas summertime I buried her
The ground was hard and dry as bone
Merciless, the scorching heat of fiery midday sun,
beat down on parched and arid soil.
No breath of wind, no sign of life or mortal toil;
I was quite alone.

The hole we'd dug two days before.
With clank and hiss, hydraulic arms and iron claw
scoured down into that hard and unforgiving ground.
Of nature's music not a sound.

Through the shimmering haze of heat,
ropes burning into hand.
I watched her slowly settle,
to her final resting place beneath my feet,
and memories all came flooding back
of summers past and flowers in the meadow
of a green and pleasant land.
And bitter tears flowed down my cheek.
But unlike sweet and gentle rain,
they only added to the pain.
No flowers now, just thistle, dock and nettle.

And then from nowhere, billowing and black,
a candyfloss of clouds appeared.
As if to celebrate - or mock - my loss
torrential rain poured down and filled the hole right to the very top.
And buoyant to the last my beloved, up did pop
as if to have one last gasp of air
and protest at the fact that death, until now dusty
had changed its mind to make her bones go rusty.

Ben Corde

Like A River

An occasional raft passes
On this calm stretch
Silent rafters, their fervour
Reserved for rapids ahead

I recall an old melody
To the drone of dragonflies
Drowned at times by chatter
Of approaching village boys

The river sustains life
Beneficiaries all
The dragonflies and I
The boys for their brimming pots

Privy to many a confessions
Warm the embrace for me
When few moments of solitude
At the riverbanks, I seek

An angst-ridden teardrop
En-route to meet the sea
Tinkle of the waters ensures
An immediate relief

An inadvertent memory of you
Catches me off guard
It inspires a little prayer
Teardrops, unbefitting now

Peace, a constant companion
And your smile, an eternal refuge
Joy a second nature, like this river
Yours be an everlasting youth

Aditya Nabial

Farewell My Lovely

My toothless wonder's left me,
he went away today.
Tho I pleaded for his sparing
we both knew he could not stay.
For seventeen years we've been companions,
he was always a delight.
Now his light has been extinguished
I've stepped from day to night.
I had kissed him on his little nose,
whispered farewell to my little friend.
I held him as he breathed his last,
Knew his life was at an end.
Was told that time shall do the healing,
said, 'I don't want to hear that now.
Right now I can't live without him,
for with a broken heart I don't know how.'

Rosie Hues

Twinkle

As the sun spreads a hello over the pillow
Stretching out into morning
As our day is dawning
My eyes creeping
Lazily dreaming
One open
then two
I see you
and your twinkles
your smiling eyes and wrinkles
Our love starts the day.

Natalie Williams

To You

A sharp arrow hit me in the back
and its metal point reached deep in my heart.
Now I lie down bleeding from within
and I don't know if I can make it before I begin.

No matter how hard I try to take the arrow out
all I can do is shout.
Shout with words that no one but God can hear
and all day long I cry without shedding a single tear.

Sometimes, somehow I manage to get away
and even forget the pain I struggle with every day.
But that's just until the next morning comes
when I see the one who makes my bleeding heart pound.
Then my body starts shivering in pain again
and all I want to do is speed up in the fast lane.

Numerous times I have tried to pull the arrow out
but could never really reach out.
O, how much I want to ease the pain
and make it disappear like a winter rain.

I pray about it every day
hoping that the pain will go away.
Yes, I know that to any torment there is an end
but now is the moment I need to find a vent.

If there is a woman you love, who loves you, appreciate her!

Atanas Atanasov

Angel

I met you one night in the rain and moonlight
Your name I'd forgotten in a tangle of fights
You came to me slow across ramps of black snow
That winter was bitter but you know I know

Your alias was alien your looks were a show
Your heart was a glass jaw, you fell at each blow
Tragedy was comic in a dark sort of way
Every time you died you woke the next day

Listen now again, as I spell it out slow
You got what you wanted now you won't go
You're living in sin down in sunny Mexico
Your man still loves you and the wee bambino

You would like to fight it all over again
But hash and tequila gold still kill the pain
And Jesus isn't such a bad man to the sick and the lame
You still bow your head when you hear His good name

John Harkin

Footprints In The Clouds

Footprints in the clouds, heading for me
A vision, an angel, it is my love I see
Beautiful candy tuft footprints at play
Directed toward me, on course this day

Footprints on a beach, two sets, one line
Ending in body imprints, passionate time
Footprints in my heart give a sweet glow
Every time my angel has to leave or go

Footprints little flutters, angels imprints
Leave my eyes, with a rose-coloured tint
Footprints in clouds, journeying to home
A vision, an angel, of the love I often loan

Christopher Slater

My Love Is Beautiful

Oh yes, nought but strawberries are her lips,
Her skin is white - as pale as thick whipped cream,
Golden thread - that's her hair - flows past her hips,
Her smile, made of light, is a blinding beam.
Her eyes are bright stars lighting the dark night,
They draw every lost traveller near,
And her face is such a breathtaking sight,
With her rosy cheeks and fair eyes - so clear.
Her locks, the same colour as the red sun,
That sets when the dazzling day turns old,
So beautiful that they can't fail to stun,
Any man that sees her, or so I'm told . . .
Oh, her beauty is the best in the land,
I am amongst the men that want her hand.

Maria Dixon

Russia With Love

Counting hours, counting ways
Setting out, seeking a way

Love you maybe
Love you today

Sensual meetings
Your hand in mind

Soldier on alone
I am with you

Let me be your Valentine
Russia - with love!

Stella Thompson

A Lifetime Of Love

The greatest treasure I have had all my life
Could not be anything other than my wife
We both saw service and courted during the war
A honeymoon was delayed until there was war no more
Married in a bombed out church in World War Two
From that day forward our love just grew and grew
When buying our house with finances rather short
She went out to work and our home was soon bought
We worked as a team to get our priorities right
Getting through crises when money was tight
We were blessed with a daughter and son
Both achieved good careers and were full of fun
The years have rolled by, children have left the nest
We now take long holidays with only brief rest
In time grandchildren to both of them were born
She was there at their bedside the very next morn
And as life goes on great-grandchildren came
Her heart was full and they were loved the same
Over the years she has protected the family with pride
Together we have battled life side by side
Now in our twilight years we have downsized
A warden-assisted Wendy house is now our prize
With her health now failing she still looks grand
Now it's my turn to lend a helping hand
We have spent our life together with give and take
She still remains my lover, wife and my mate.

Leonard Butler

Why?

I've cried my tears for thirty years
Alone . . .
So when I meet nostalgia
I'm wondering then where you are
And if you, too, remember?
(perhaps 'our film', 'our song')
It just tugs at my heartstrings
Reminding me
Again - I don't 'belong'

There's no shared mem'ries to discuss;
No friends to be recalled
No laughter at the times we've shared

No strengthening, too, of family ties
Just memories of such sad times
Of months filled up with dreadful lies.

For thirty years I've wondered 'why'?
'What if', 'maybe' - and such
Why do I feel so empty -
Why did I lose so much?

Edna Sparkes

Closing The Circle

There are many circles in life
Some not seen at the time
Mine came from my late partner
Thro' the mists of time
A part of you, dear one, I am going to miss
When Mr Woods, your accountant is through
He has always been very kind
So will soon, bid him adieu
I shall feel completely alone
And it's worrying me so
Perhaps you'll be on hand somewhere
I know you've said, not to worry so,
But I do, as into the unknown, I will go
Without you.
It will be the end of an era
With the Queen's Head too
As long ago, it was my grandfather's pub
For farmers it was said
What's inside, I do not know (I still don't)
Giving me an idea of long ago.
Can see men, in their brown garb,
Doffing caps and hats going thro' the door
For a well-earned drink, with a neighbour
Talking farming, weather, cattle, sometimes mowing
Quaffing ale, soon to be going
Home, to their wife and family
To fall asleep and then to be
Getting up early, work thro' the day
Even earlier at harvest time, just
Like my grandfather, and very little pay
Hoping weather would stay fine, for the day.
My grandfather was such a lovely man
Had blue eyes, just like you
Always smiling, another thing too
Which was exactly like you.
Always had such patience with me
Perhaps I would talk to the bullocks, you see
Bringing them grass, twigs of green

Would sing to them, when allowed
New ones, might be afraid
I was not afraid of these big animals
Behind their mangers of many angles
In the cattle shed
Can see them now, all big and brown
With huge eyes, tossing heads
Snuffling in the birgs amidst the chaff
Blowing it about, would cause a laugh.
I nearly grew up to be a farming 'gal'
Sewing caught me in its thrall
Then I met you
That was my biggest thrill of all
So like my grandfather, in so many ways
Especially with those lovely, smiling, blue eyes
That was my fate
Old memories, have just been recalled
Back to 1937, with years in-between
Incidentally, the year, you were born.
Seemed as though my fate was sealed
By the Queen's Head House.
You see, my grandfather, used to hire a driver and car
To see his sister in a village yearly (lady being ill)
Taking me along for company
Visit over, then drive to the Queen's Head
Being only eight, had to wait in the car instead
As of today, it is and was your accountant's office
Still with worn grey steps, I remembered so well
Then you dear one, taking me there
At the thought, causing my eyes to well
With tears.

Mabel Deb Moore

Otherness

On a cold, dark night,
I was sitting still, resting,
On a crowded train -
You were both sitting opposite me.
I think you were eighteen, or nineteen . . .

All was quiet in the carriage.
Silence, and stillness, and calmness -
People read their newspapers.
A man kept eating fruit pastilles,
One after the other.

Commuter train, London to Fleet for me.
For you, I didn't know.
You both intrigued me, I admit.
I was aware of your every moves -
All about you was nice.

One of you read a newspaper,
The other one glanced at it from the side.
At some point you tried silently,
Together to do the crossword puzzle -
A quiet, gentle moment.

Then you both laughed spontaneously
At something you were reading.
Two brothers, I was wondering . . .
Or just close friends?
Probably not, possibly not.

Before Fleet, one of you
Put his arm around the other's shoulders.
We got off the train together -
Outside, you both walked
Holding hands.

Claire-Lyse Sylvester

A House For My Mum

I've bought a house for my mum
It didn't cost me a whole lot
I would spend anything though
It's got everything she needs
She will live there forever
A good roof over her head
Roses in the back garden
Hanging plants outside her doors
Don't think she'll ever feel bad
I will be praying for her
No tears running down her cheek
No complaints crowding her mind
I've plans for her she might like
I'll buy her things every day
I long for her to love me
Only that would set me free

Muhammad Khurram Salim

Starstruck

He never was my life, his company was fleeting
But there he is at every dawn and every morning greeting
I shield my eyes on sunny days and glimpse the dazzling sea
And see him where the sea meets land, just far too far for me
But in dark corners of the night when memories drift afar
I reach into the evening sky and touch his brilliant star.

Margaret Whitehead

And Now

And now
I pick up mirror shards.
Walking on ice watery-thin,
slip cut fingertips.

What, why, is,
for everything.
no more yes, this is,
for me.

My washed eyes
don't like what they see.
I am feeding myself
to uncertainty.

Other eyes mould into yours;
I give into blood welling desire
in a search for
lost you.

Every day
has become your gravestone.
Each reminder, a relic.

Time has never been so foreign -
it slows with each dying minute.

Naomi Portman

Love Asleep

And love it came on me asleep
Too soon to see the cares and woes
While I saw the object that it stood
So many times in the world of the past
How lighted it upon the world
So many things to see it through
And spoke the challenges
Changes too
That set about the behemoth that stood
The life that stood beyond the pale

And stood by the all-forgiving truth
Where stood wherefore
Did it but see
The only thing to give was me
For nothing that could
Give it life
Stood in the path
That others trod
But love arose
And love stood firm

Love conquered
And ran its turn
While I mere mortal
Stood its grace
And ran on the whims and wiles
To the end that it placed no time
But went as the dew
Sundered to the winds
From whence it came

Alasdair Sclater

12 -7

Early morning 2am,
He returns to a spinning hotel room,
Silent and alone,
He dreams of her.

She envelops his consciousness,
Reaching out to him from somewhere distant.
He imagines what could be,
Given a different night,
Another life,
Another way.

He wonders why it's not the case,
That she's here with him now,
A fluke of time and space.

Another evening spent with her,
Somehow so perfect,
So beautiful,
So vivid before him,
Yet, not so clear,
Intangible.
An entrancing enigma,
So close,
Yet so distant.
An impossibility.

Like the view from the aeroplane on the flight here,
Looking down to the snowy peaks of the mountains below.
Rising towards him through the clouds.
He remembers touching the window with his finger,
Tracing the contours of ancient rocks below him,
Unable to reach them.

He sighs and slumps on the bed,
Closes his eyes,
And re-enacts this evening,
In his mind.

He loves talking to her,
The others fade away when he's with her.
He leans towards her,
And is engulfed by her aura.
What do the others think?
Do they wonder what's happening to him?
He wonders.

Why this magnetism?
Why this mysticism?
Drawing him in,
Like a gravitational pull,
A spiritual quest,
Over which he has no control,
Like clouds wrapping themselves naturally,
Unconsciously,
Around those mountains,
Clinging on to spite the wind,
Trying to tear them apart.

She'll be flying home tomorrow.
He has to see her one more time before she leaves.

Mike Wride

Feelings . . .

My heart cries a thousand words,
My tears are filled with anger
And my mind with everlasting hatred.

I am left alone to cry a thousand words on my own,
Just because I have a fight with my sister.

The moon awakens and so does my heart,
Hoping for forgiveness and a fresh start.
Sometimes it comes,
Sometimes it doesn't.

Nothing is certain!

But what is certain is that . . .
No matter what the situation is
Or whose fault it is,

I will be blamed for the pains and sorrows of all;
As being the youngest is the biggest crime of all.

Sonia Kauser

Valentine's Day

The solitary square white envelope lay on the mat
By the front door. Bending painfully,
She picked it up and took it into the back room,
Where she slit the envelope with the little silver knife
Which had been her father's
And took out the card.

Tracing the big red heart with her finger
She admired the garland of forget-me-nots.
They had always been her favourite flowers,
With their simple blue faces.

He always remembered, that brave soldier
Who had been so ready to fight for Queen and Country.

Opening the card she blinked away tears as she read
'To my darling Sylvia - always in my heart'.

Later, she went into the cramped front parlour
And taking a big biscuit tin, with a picture of the Queen on it,
She laid the card inside, on top of the others.
Looking at the strong rounded letters on the envelope
She remembered she had always been proud of her handwriting.

Gillian Peall

Love Birds

Sitting after breakfast
In my chair as is my usual wont
I spied outside my window
A magpie just out front
I said the usual greetings
As one does when seeing just one magpie
Then watched him breaking off a twig
And soar off in the sky
He did almost a full circle
Landing back whence he came
Then his lady friend or wife
Did exactly the same
He gave her the twig in her beak
They then kissed and cuddled a while
They sat close together as lovebirds
Planning together
Who knows with a smile?

Daphne Fryer

Mother's Love

What is a mother's love you may ask?
One who rarely complains at any task.
Her love she gives unselfishly
At our faults says, 'What will be, will be.'

Her tasks are many without much reward.
She gives of herself of her own accord.
Mum meets everyone's needs and that's a fact.
Neglects her own and shows immense tact.

Ignores our faults that we show.
Gives her permission when we go.
Out of her life, into the unknown.
Leaving her with the thought, how quick they have grown.

We make the mistakes, do a 'Black bin bag parade'
Her love for us will never fade.
She accepts us back with arms open wide.
Picks up the bits and nurses hurt with pride.

She somehow 'mends' us and it makes sense.
Mum's not so quick to 'sit on the fence'.
She works out our problems, gives good advice.
Whether or not it is taken, she's always nice.

What we would do without her, I know not.
A great deal of her caring we may have forgot.
Her purpose it is true, Mum will try to mend.
Her love is constant she's forever our friend.

Ellen Spiring

Resisted Moments

A desire in the look
Glance better to ignore
A smile designed to wrong foot
Gently draw.

A smoothness in the voice
Wiser not to hear
A smoothness that rejoice
To draw one near.

A genial touch on the shin
To make one wondering why
Puts the mind in a spin
It's better to deny.

It's folly to resist
Deny oneself a lifetime of bliss.

Bryan G Clarke

The Heart In The Snow

Sighing, looking out on a snowy landscape
Howgill fells pass by in silence
Immersing themselves to the smothered occupancy of snow
Trees to the left on the great fell form a heart shape
Black limbs against the pristine whiteness
A perfect, timeless shape
Did someone plant the trees especially for their lover?
A stark posture of a conscious silhouette
The trees invaluable, intimate reassurance of submissively being
The subtle planting, inhabiting a piece of fell, their lover's vulnerability
Is endlessly transparent on such a bleak, abandoned hillside
An indulgent elegance evident, the unbroken heart shape,
Its diversity eternal to the seasons
Enriching souls assurance of the transforming grace of love
Which can liberate and remain faithful forever
In the solitude of the trees

Hilary Jean Clark

Edward's Music

I can hear music.
This music is full of love
It renews my heart.
I come to Jesus.
I ask for nothing greater.
Leave me at His side.
He has rescued me.
He has freed me from danger.
There is no peril.
It happens to me!
It's extraordinary!
Music surrounds me!
Edward sings to me.
He sings to me with closed lips.
He lulls me to sleep.
He can sing so well.
He is a special angel.
This sound is gentle.
Edward sings of love!
Edward also sings of joy!
My emotions glow!
There's a room for us.
It is private, just for two.
He plays lullabies.
His music of love.
I could ask for nothing more.
Edward is too kind.
Springtime's water drops,
They relieve me of my pain.
His music does, too.

Laraine Smith

House Of Queens

O Lydia the greatest,
Likened to a Greek goddess,
Of fortune, fame and high office,
O powerful sovereign ruler,

O bring the legions of Rome,
With your armies and chariots,
With laurels, your diadem and crown,
Bedazzled by rubies, sapphires and emeralds,

O come resplendent queen,
So compelling a woman of love,
Inside the house of queens,
As you gaze at that perpetual midnight star,

O beauteous creature, O Epicurean woman,
Madame's room decorated with white roses,
The glorification of love,
Maddened with fury, a spiritual masterpiece above,

As you walk across a beautiful Roman mosaic,
Surrounded by nymphs and cherubs,
Inside the Pantheon temple,
The oracle of Delphi, on a summertime's day,

Ordained with greatness, the parliament of queens,
Inspired with opulence and brilliance,
Omnipotent, graceful with nobility,
While meandering besides a fan of peacocks,

Their beautiful plumage on show,
Like an aristocratic beauty,
Illustrating immense power,
Imperial English monarch,

O immortal distinguished woman,
The bewitching legacy of Queen Lydia.

James Stephen Cameron

Winter Wonderland

Dawn breaking, Xmas Eve, leaving Wickford for Harrogate
with courier Newmarket Holidays
snow-encased 4-star Holiday Inn - very comfortable rooms,
Christmas card and present on the bed
Nottingham for lunch famous for Robin Hood in Sherwood Forest
Harrogate - visited the Spa, Pump Room and Aunt Betty's Tea Room

3pm watched the Queen and ate Christmas cake with coffee
And taken to Ripon Cathedral
Lewis Caroll's father, a Canon inspired by misericord carvings
And 'Alice in Wonderland'
Sheet copper sculptured statues by Harold Gosney
St Wilfred - 634 -709 - founder of cathedral
Toured Skipton Castle - 1090 built by Robert de Romille a Norman Baron

Clifford family granted property from Edward II - 1310
Lady Anne Clifford planted the yew tree 1659 in the Conduit Court
has medieval kitchen, banqueting hall and watchtower
visited Lincoln which has the 'Green Dragon' pub

Dick Turpin's famous ride London to York
- Bracebridge Heath on Black Bess - 1737
Landlord Silas Serappe arrested for goods stolen -
sentenced to 20 years Lincoln jail
Hotel with evening entertainment, Andy Greeves sings
'Never felt like singing the Blues'
'Sleigh Bells', 'Chestnuts roasting on an open fire'
turkey and mistletoe, Santa's on his way

Ventriloquist duck 'Lewis' sang 'Don't laugh at me'
Laurie Bennett sang 'You make me feel so young'
'Some day I'm going to write the story of my life'
'Welcome to my world', 'Step into my heart'

'With these hands I will cling to you'
'All my love, all my kisses', 'We're having a party'
Sheep roam in the dales - beautiful countryside
mallards, coots, Canadian geese,
tufted birds, heather, grouse, curlews
yellow rockrose, purple thyme
wood anemones - memories of a wonderful break
Nice people
This glorious land of English heritage.

Patricia Turpin

The Passing Of Time

The years have all gone by,
Yet still we are together,
When we first started out,
Did we believe it was forever?
Many hardships and troubles,
We have indeed weathered,
To each other we still are tethered,
Romance gestures there were few.
But to each other we have remained true,
The children are now all grown,
With partners of their own,
Life still busy though our family has flown,
We seemed to spend a lot of time alone,
Are we dreading the day
When we have to live on our own?

Pauline Uprichard

Fairy Tale

I thought we were
Reading the same story

Presumed we were
On the same page

Slowly I realised it
Was different chapters

Now I sit alone
In a dimly-lit café

Trying to figure out
Why the fairy tale

Didn't end
'Happily ever after'

Gaelynne Pound

You And I

Together forever,
Till the day we die,
Our love has grown,
All others we defy.

A holy pact,
Rings on our fingers,
Never to destroy,
Our love will linger.

Jonathan Simms

Wedding Anniversary

The ups and downs of marriage
Are living's ebb and flow
A marriage has a rhythm
Most high and then a bit of low

Our marriage has that pattern
But comes each dawn anew
We closer came together
Our love just grew and grew

Our wedlock made my living
Our marriage served me right
In receiving I am grateful
And giving's my delight

The years are passing quickly
Days quickly pass on through
That speed it does not matter
Because they're shared with you

I'm grateful for our children
In turn their children too
But most of all I'm grateful
For our marriage dearest you.

Ray Ryan

Together

After another restless night she'd overslept,
At some point during endless long hours she had wept,
Horrible thoughts into night dreams had swiftly crept.

But once morning arrived she again felt the love,
From family on Earth and those up above,
Once he called her honey bun, she cooed like a dove.

In early evening he would leave to go to work,
Lowly paid employment from which he could not shirk,
When serving drunken patrons he would often smirk.

He longed to be home giving his lover a kiss,
Wished their daily lives did not have to be like this,
But knew that if he resigned; his wage they would miss.

Both decided that a new year meant a new start,
He'd look for a day job, at night needn't be apart,
They were neither ruled by old heads but by young hearts.

Susan Mullinger

War

Heroes Helping

The glorious dead!
There is no glory in death
But much more
Much, much, more
Remembrance
Respect
And yes!
Gratitude above all
Could I be so brave
To give my life
And all I have for
The Queen's shilling?
Damn it!
There is glory
In death.

Jamise

War

W orking hard for your country
A ttacking the enemy side
R ationing back at home

I ncoming bombs
S tarvation in the concentration camps

F eeling the danger
I ncoming enemies
G unfire raging through
H itting the enemy planes
T rampling horses
I n major battles
N o more survivors
G oing through hell

War is fighting!

Ben Ball

This Wasted Landscape

This wasted landscape blown all to hell,
The tortured earth answering death's grim bell.
Spider-like trees twist in agony into the grey sky,
No branches, no leaves for on the ground they lie.
The earth churned up by some giant's plough,
Will the grass and flowers ever come back somehow?
A world devoid of a spectrum of colour,
Greys and blacks make this godforsaken place duller.

From Death's Wood five downcast figures appear,
Their shabby uniforms, their faces too numbed to show fear.
Shuffling across the duckboards like they are but in a dream,
Across muddy water, dark, stinking like putrefying cream.
Getting nearer now, their faces look aged beyond their years,
Stunned, zombie-like, no longer able to shed any tears.
Too exhausted to acknowledge a single shell overhead,
No cares left, their emotions cast out, forgotten in some shed.

And on they go seemingly lost in the Devil's horror show,
Where are they shuffling along to? Only they know.
Just five soldiers lost in the war to end all wars,
Just five of many lost in the Grim Reaper's tours.
Into the clammy mist the figures now fade,
Swallowed up, their debt to the war now paid.
Now only on a monochrome photo, they exist forever,
A symbol of Man's primeval war-like endeavour.

Alan Sturdey

No-One's Land, No-Man's-Land

Kitchener's call to arms, patriots, the young, the unwary enlist,
home for Christmas to a hero's welcome, empty promises sold,
young boys, nay cannon fodder, many lost in the mist,
defenders of our great country, like our kings centuries afore, so bold.

Into trenches they march, the front line, unimaginable horror awaits,
before them lies a desolate, godforsaken landscape, no birdsong, no trees,
if Hell doth exist then surely this must be Hell, each awaits his fate,
lookouts stand guard in a shell hole waist deep in water, starts to freeze.

A broken land where no man nor beast should care to recall,
torrential rain then adds to the misery, thick mud, dawn, a whistle blows,
sick with fear and fright, over the top, bayonets fixed, so very many fall,
walking headlong into murderous gunfire, no hiding, no cover, machine gun mows.

The dying who litter the field call for their mother, stretcher bearers the cry,
every human instinct would have said, run, hide, bombs and mortars maim,
friends, comrades, never found, lost to eternity, devoured by the mud, deathly sky,
after witnessing such horrors how could life ever possibly be the same?

Mercilessly, incessantly, shells fall, deafening, frightening, the very earth shakes,
shocked survivors tumble into enemy positions, vicious close-quarter combat ensues,
huge rats feast upon the spoils, the unfortunate from their nightmare awakes,
mutilated corpses hang from the barbed wire, scenes never shown on the news.

Barely recognisable lines of humanity once proud uniforms, now only rags,
eyes bandaged, arms outstretched, poisoned by gas, blind led by the blind,
overworked medics, surgeons knee-deep in amputations, blood, morale sags,
the great war, the war to end all wars, never again shall we see its kind.

Michael Hartshorne

March

March my Son.
March forward, march onward,
March up the long roads,
March down brutal paths,
March over sands,
March left and march right.
March wearing your helmet,
March with your rucksack on your back,
March with your rifle by your side.
March forward in the cold rain,
March on in the hot sun,
March while obeying orders.
March my Son with a smile,
March on with a sigh.
March towards waiting trucks,
March onto ships, to conflict and to strain.
March on my Son, March.
March as we wave goodbye,
March as we wipe tears from our eyes,
March on my brave Son,
March on to war.
March on.

Edna Colby

War Is . . .

War is burning
fire, lava and infernal
destroying Hell itself.

War is destruction
debris, burn and destroy
exploding buildings.

War is invading
power, glory and greed
taking countries.

War is poisoning
assassinating, killing, murdering
taking people's lives.

We should destroy war!

Elliot McSheen

War Is . . .

War is bleeding
soldiers falling and dying,
over the bloody battlefield.

War is bombing
buildings smoking and collapsing,
onto trembling civilians and cars.

War is killing
slaughtering civilians,
dying for what you believe.

War is sinking
battleships exploding,
wounded marines drowning.

Reece Nicholson

What Is War?

What is war?
War is hatred, hell,
War is anger, fury,
War is sadness, depression.

What is blood?
Blood is a river of fear,
Blood is lava exploding through the ground,
Blood is poison going in instead of out.

What is death?
Death is the last blow on a dandelion,
Death is a leaf turning brown,
Death is the last bark from a dog.

What is war?
War is hatred, hell,
War is anger, fury,
War is sadness, depression.

Don't let war happen.

James Bibby

Reflex Action

A hand groped in the darkness,
disturbing my sleep.
Split second timing!
That's what they taught me.
If it moves . . . kill it!

So I did, using the knife
I'd placed beneath my pillow.
Now I sit in silence, staring
at my wife's limp body.

No one, prepared me for that.

Paul Kelly

Hues In Love And War

He watched her walk, to a taupe stiletto beat
Her rose cheeks rosier in love's blushing heat,

Pink her lips quivered, as she called out his name
Spellbound his ruby-red heart fell for this dame,

Yellow rays shone down on her beautiful hair
Then golden sunbeams danced and entwined the pair,

White her wedding dress when they married that day
Grey were the clouds when he had to go away,

Khaki was the colour of his uniform
Orange sun glowed, as he went to war at dawn,

Red, blue and white his flag, on his battleship
Which sailed alone on an azure, one-way trip,

Crashing waves threw him on a sand-coloured beach
That some ivory-faced comrades, did not reach,

Steel-blue was the look in his enemie's eyes
Coal-black was the gunshot that streaked through the skies,

Russet were the leaves when he fell to the ground
Crimson were his fatal wounds when he was found,

Burnt umber was the mud on the battlefield
As to white angels' arms, his soul he did yield,

Green were the French hills where he was laid to rest
A vast rainbow arch, linked his east to her west,

Cream the telegram, delivered to her door
Blue was her heart that she would see him no more,

Opaque the silent tears that fell down her face
Whilst a myriad of hues helped peace take place.

Susi Howell

On The Loss Of A Son

Could I escape this raging mind which mourns the loss of one so dear
And be a whisper or a sigh, my love for him would still be clear
If I could be a roaring wind or gentle breeze just passing by
Or maybe rain that wets the earth, cascading freely from the sky
A sunbeam falling on a flower, a golden light beyond compare
I watch it, dreaming by the hour - I see it, but it isn't there
Such jealousy of fleeting things which stay a moment free of care
Such longing every moment brings - I wish I could be as nowhere
Why do I fantasise and dream - why wish to be a pale moonbeam
Why envy each ethereal light, not sleeping through a tortured night
Imaginations without end, why do I wish these things could be?
The answer is quite simple friend - it's much too painful to be me.

Dorothy Blakeman

Enduring Freedom

'Three children playing with a shell were blown
to bits in Helmand Province yesterday'.
Back home three others mourn a father's death.
'Murder of innocence!' the headline shouts.
'Where is he now?' one asks. 'In Heaven, love,'
they say. 'With freedom there's a price to pay.'
Everything's relative, God only knows.
Will it bear fruit this cross of sacrifice?

The town is quietened while the piper plays
'Amazing Grace'. Along High Street folk pause,
watch loved ones toss red roses at the hearse,
turn back into their lives. Graveside, Last Post
is sounding, drowns in silence at floodtide.
Six riflemen fire blanks. There's no reply.

Peter Branson

War-Torn Afghanistan

The woundings and the killings
Of our troops in war-torn Afghanistan
Is beyond all comprehension:
As they bring the coffins of their comrades home
They in turn bear the same fate
The same sad conclusion.
For every minute of every day
They are maimed or slain
And their loved ones are tragically left
Grief-stricken and forlorn
For their lives shall never be the same again;
We question the right of the government
To keep sending our soldiers there
Ill-equipped as they are
To deal with the situation;
Hence, bring them out we cry in unison
Allow them to be reunited with their families
For enough is enough
This is the sane and only solution.

Gwyneth E Scott

This World, My World, Our World

Rain spills gently from a neutral sky
Neither dark nor threatening, just still
As it opens its heart and cries silently
On a world of apparent sameness that is no more.

My world looks serene, with pretty houses
Fields of green and summer sounds
Of birds singing, hidden in green-leafed trees
Away from my stalking tiger on window sill

Yet my world is no longer this, not as I knew
I ponder this as I look across dampening valley
The façade of tranquillity is breaking
Crumbling, cracking, being rent at every angle

My life, this gentle British life,
Is being rent and we, no longer spectators.
What makes mankind so terribly unkind?
What makes belief in a loving God turn to murderous intent?

What in Heaven's name can we do to heal
To stop the bitterness and cruel blind faith
From destroying our world, our lives, our peace?
Tell me God, I'm listening, tell me and it shall be done.

Polly Leschenko

A Letter

Mr Prime Minister, behind your Black Door,
have you ever been summoned to war,
seen the destruction of homes and lives
and witnessed the terror in people's eyes?

What do you think of when drinking your tea,
all sorts of policies, but no thought of me,
whilst we watch friends walking by
hidden bombs ready to blow them sky high?

You can't begin to know how it feels to see
half a face in the mirror and realise 'that's me'.
Lots of your soldiers minus, arms and legs,
are supposed to feel lucky that they are not dead!

Doctors say we should be referred to see
a person to give us therapy.
Although we try and tell you our plight,
our dreams remain real every night

And the reality of this war, you see,
is the knowing that it shouldn't be.

Eda Hughes

Normandy, As Seen Through Fred's Eyes

Saddened eyes reflect a quiet mind now rudely awakened
By returning memories seeped in violent pain
We sit in silence upon this golden sand
Many of your long-lost friends begin to appear again
I am witnessing battle through your eyes
A proud soldier of advancing years
How many ghostly bodies lie strewn and still?
Seen now through vision blurred by heartfelt tears
Inform yet unbeaten you tell us all a hurtful tale
Of young soldiers, sailors, death and fear
The endless noise of guns and cries
Did they fall to their death before your eyes?
Cry once more for pain that still feels raw
Each droplet a memory of the victims of war
Bootless feet tested the strength of many men
Will they ever see their homes again?
No end in sight, blood-red skies above
You fought to turn selfish hatred into love
Guns are blazing as vessels try to land
Death becomes each grain of sand
Memories of bloodshed have paled your ageing skin
Bubbles of anger erupting deep within
Confusion clouds your crumpled face
Senseless murder and human waste
Around you there are smiles of joy
Our life is different from when you were a boy
The churning waves before you devoured with ease
Violent horror unknown by me creating scarlet seas
I now offer a prayer for those that are lost
A gift of peace I hope they see
Wars are fought through greed and hate
Tolerance of difference is a non-existent trait
I feel a need to stop and turn
For I cannot bear to see
The pain you suffered for my life

Without ever knowing me
What lessons have we learned over time?
Not the necessity for peace
We need to show tolerance of all mankind
Selfish greed and unreasonable hate must cease
If another world war should happen to be
The youth of today would not help my family or me
Values and morals are sadly in decline
The role of cannon fodder is not for any child of mine
War is the colour of blood and night
Man against man in a mindless fight
Stop and think before bullets fly again
Of families left with life-long pain

Lynn Elizabeth Noone

Daddy Is A Star

Your daddy is a star,
He's up there in the sky.
He went to help some people,
He didn't mean to die!
He had to do his duty,
He had to fight a war,
When men in suits knocked on the door,
I knew what it was for!
I need you to be brave,
I need you to be strong,
Remember Daddy loved you so,
Even if this all seems wrong.
A boy without his daddy,
It weren't his time to go,
But he will always watch over you,
And that's all you need to know!

Hazel Brawn

One Future Day

All nations know the bitter pain of war,
their history has been stained by human blood,
internal and external has raged the foe.

Such conflicts have affected young and old,
for none escape the costly price that's paid
in terms of heartache, sorrow, pain or death.

The parents mourn the treasured son they've lost,
the widow's heart is robbed of wedded bliss,
the fatherless can no more greet their dad.

The list of casualties each day increase
and nursing hands attend horrific wounds,
the trauma known that time cannot erase.

The streams of refugees reach endless length,
displaced from home with all possessions lost,
their faces marked by hopelessness and fear.

But there shall come a day when wars shall cease,
all nations live in harmony and peace
when Christ, the Prince of Peace, at last shall reign.

Until that day let's firmly trust in God,
who hates injustice, tyranny and war
but gives His grace the ills of life to bear.

Stanley Birch

The Lion And The Eagle

The lion and the eagle,
Are dancing cheek to cheek;
Was this war ever legal?
They've led us up the creek.

Come see the burning bush,
Come hear the trumpets blare;
Throughout the land they push,
Oppose them if you dare.

'Let's topple the dictator,
Export democracy;
We'll silence any traitor,
Who dares to disagree.'

Our lads are in Iraq,
Join in the battle boys;
They press home their attack,
Back home kids rattle toys.

From Downing Street to White House,
The corridors of power;
Cheri is just the right spouse,
And Laura is a flower.

Man's greed and love of money,
Is a spreading, cancerous root;
False prophets speak words of honey,
You'll know them by their fruit.

Weapons of mass destruction.
That never even existed;
Have caused a seismic ruction,
And got our land blacklisted.

'Don't show them any mercy,
We've got to get their oil;
Our cars are ever thirsty,
Invade the Muslim soil.'

Andrew Stephenson

Sacrifice

I give you a red rose to remember.
Our people brave and true.
Who went to war for this country.
And gave up their lives for you.

I give you a red rose to remember.
The sacrifices given unselfishly.
They fought and died for this country.
So our world would always be free.

I give you a red rose to remember.
Those women standing hand in hand.
Who lost their dearly loved ones.
In a strange and alien land.
And faced a future bleak and lonely.
So we could walk with pride
And for this noble cause.
Thousands of our finest died.

I give you a red rose to remember.
Not to let their sacrifice be in vain.
Now we must be brave and fight.
A different war again.

Some politicians cynical and corrupt.
Have given away the freedom these boys sought.
Have taken away many of the rights.
For which these brave boys fought.

So take this red rose and remember.
That we must not let them down.
We must fight for the things they died for.
Our democracy, our freedom and our Crown.

Pamela Matthews

Farewell To The Homeland (Ethnic Cleansing)

Goodbye dear haunts I've known
my once familiar home
with heavy heart
I leave for paths unknown

Farewell dear ancient sites
inspirers of our skills,
I shall return
to see you in my dreams

Some day, post war perhaps
they'll let our people back
to claim our land
and cultivate your soil

We'd be a team again
set free to put down roots
and sow the fruits
the plunderers have plucked

But now distraught we part
our shattered lives on edge
from shells and slaughter
violence all around

They've burned our homes and farms
and brutally attacked
our people who unarmed
now flee to live

Yet peace was all we sought
To let our children know
Our customs, skills, beliefs
That help them grow.

Rosemary Keith

The Inquisition

Blood ran down the Houses of Parliament
In rivulets, strong and bold and bitter.
Painful tears of life and love and laughs lost.
Forever gone. Gone into nothingness.

Ashes to ashes, dust to dust.

The open flesh-wound of society,
Forever present, forever unhealed.
Clear for all to see the toll taken,
The price paid by courageous beating hearts.

Ashes to ashes, dust to dust.

Now beloved - no longer our loved ones,
They are over there, never to return.
A false command, a broken leadership.
The air thickens as the smoke surrenders.

Ashes to ashes, dust to dust.

Committed to memory, they waver.
The forgotten fallen in a fraught fight,
Etched to our country as we forget them.
They fade away into the black abyss.

Ashes to ashes, dust to dust.

A supernova in our consciousness,
The ill-fated of the ill-thought and ill-equipped.
Shaming and shameful to each and all
Though we try to forget, try to ignore.

Ashes to ashes, dust to dust.

The debt rising, the interest mounting up,
Of a war we did not want to enter,
Now a toll and tax we cannot escape,
The price heavier than the victory.

Ashes to ashes, dust to dust.

Ria Landrygan

The Other Men 1914-1918

Somehow they're still with us - the other men,
Of course you cannot see them
Except in the old newsreels
Laughing as men will and angels never do.

You see them queuing at recruitment stations,
Happy sinners, innocent as newborn babies
About this great thing
That has come upon them.

You see them from the carriages
Of the steam engines, heads stuck
Out of open windows, arms waving
To impress the jolly cameraman.

It's so long ago now with no one
Left to say they were there.
A few years ago some very old men
Remembering when they were green as grass.

Grass will green the earth,
Flowers will bloom and fade,
Erosion will fill in and soften contours,
Taking away the rough edges of steel.

Robert William Lockett

War With Honour

(Dedicated to John Munton, born in Norfolk, 1834 and who joined No 7 Company 12th Battalion, Royal Artillery Regiment, and served in the Crimean war from 17th October 1854 to 8th September 1855)

'God bless, may the Lord keep you safe and well'
were the cries, as we left to fond farewells.
Trepidation grew, I felt a mounting fear.
The rising swell of the tide swamped the boat,
as the Crimean coastline drew near.

We wake to the sound of Russian guns, no food,
just despair of the cold dark night.
It's been twelve long hours of constant fatigue,
mud, filth and frostbite

Untreated wounds from constant fire, rot, gangrenous and hot.
We are not able to reach aid or help, vermin gains as
bodies die, a voice is heard, 'Meagre rations boys,
that's your lot.'

Some say she's an angel from Heaven working
to save us wounded souls.
The Lady with the Lamp draws near, a saviour who
prolongs the agony, no treatment for the freedom
from pain, just bare rations in unwashed bowls.

Once great beasts in friendly places a Drover's
companion put to the plough.
Now skeletal shapes upon the horizon, starved and
tired, broken of spirit.
Struggling with cannon as rotting hooves sink
deeper into the slough.

No gas, no aeroplanes, no looting or suicidal bombs.
Just guns and us in appalling conditions,
because we were fighting fair.
We fought with honour, camaraderie and
the good Lord's prayer.

Mai Clarke-Edden

Message To The World, What's The Point?

Soldiers sacrificing souls,
What's the point?
To lose a limb or a joint,
Just one shot of a gun,
A mother loses her son,
Brave like a lion,
Until they are dying.

Armies appearing armed,
What's the point?
No one to hug,
Nowhere to run,
It's not that fun,
Why is it done?
You may be strong as an ox,
But grief comes and knocks.

Everyone everywhere be aware,
What's the point?
It's the bosses who decide,
They are tucked up inside,
Unaware of the pain,
Whilst they sip champagne,
As cold as ice,
They throw the dice.

Life lost living
What's the point?
Hit by lead,
Bang! You're dead,
All soldiers fear the sound,
The second they do they hit the ground,
You could be the best of the best,
But you might die like the rest.

What's the point?

Thomas Phillip Cottee (11)

The Great War

This was to be the carnage of the century,
A chapter in life that should have never been,
Destruction of mankind as never seen before,
A hopeless, bloody, senseless war,
Innocent young men so bravely born,
Would soon be cut down like sheaves of corn,
Field Marshall Haig's plea,
'Your country needs you now', was a far-off cry,
With no guarantee whether you live or die,
Men volunteered to do their best,
Soon the fields of Flanders would be covered in red,
Blood of the dying and those already dead,
The battlefields Ypres, Passchendaele and the Somme,
Why all this carnage, what has gone wrong?
Questions remaining for those still fighting and hanging on,
For loved ones back home would be left to mourn,
With the awakening of each new day,
So many heartaches, so many tears,
Will remain with them forever along with the passing years,
So let us not forget other wars,
For the sake of future generations, there will be no more.

Don Carpenter

The Safeguard

Though many years of my life have fled,
The memories of my childhood still linger.
When the enemy blitzed and the city bled,
And searchlight flared with frantic finger.

Children, then wished for a silver balloon,
To tether to their house tops in the night,
Or strati cloud to veil the bombers' moon,
So raiders would stay their savage blight.

Such dangers decreed that we seek safety
In hamlet and village throughout the land.
Living in abodes both simple and stately,
While Britain took, perhaps, her last stand.

Safe place, where children acquired grace,
Gone the sob of sirens that made us mute,
Or searching for a face, lost without trace,
When landmines fell earthward on a chute.

Dogfights and vapour trails scarred the sky,
As the few, fought the foe, to inflict harm.
The land must have uttered many a forlorn cry
As we lived halcyon days down on the farm.

William Carr

The Fallen Of Fromelles

My grandad was a Didekoi, a Gypsy, a travelling man,
who roamed the narrow Kentish lanes in a painted caravan.
He'd mend your pots and kettles, and carved wooden dolly pegs.
He was a dab hand with a horse and never once did beg.

A big Shire he called Plodder, pulled the small van with ease,
and time never meant anything, they ambled as they pleased.
He'd set a rabbit snare to catch a bunny for his pot,
and he knew the shady campsites near a stream if days were hot.

Plodder stood sixteen hands high, with feet as big as plates.
A gentle, willing dark bay horse, my grandad's equine mate.
He threw his weight into the traces, and gave all he was worth
Horse brasses shone upon his bridle and on his plaited girth.

Grandad was a handsome fellow as the Gypsies often are
and young girls flocked around him where he travelled near and far.
But he had eyes for no one save a dark-haired, sloe-eyed lass
who was promised him in marriage and that soon would come to pass.

But thunder rolled and dark clouds came and soon the War Gods called
young men to fight for King and country, their bravery extolled.
The mothers in every county wept as they sent their sons to war.
Few knew where their boys were sent once they left England's shore.

My grandad with the 61st Div, left England's shore behind.
He knew not what was waiting, but was calm within his mind
He knew the fighting must be done. Loved ones must be protected,
but when he landed at Fromelles 'twas worse than he expected.

The air was thick with bullets in a criss-cross grid of death.
Hundreds were mown down as they stood, ne'er chance to draw a breath.
The German forces had set up machine-gun enfilades
The Aussie boys were fighting too . . . death paid for every yard.

After the battle guns had stopped, for the battle was lost
Germans reclaimed the land that our troops recently had crossed
Over two hundred bodies the Germans took to 'Pheasant Wood'
Eight mass graves behind the German lines waited for allied blood.

We think my grandad one of them, for he never returned
His sloe-eyed lass with raven hair for many years sadly yearned

To hold him in her arms again, but it was not to be
The Didekoi, the Gypsy lad never returned you see.

But now today the fallen, who fought and died in France
have finally been found again, given a second chance
to become a part once more of their families' memories
in a cemetery built to honour them across the sea.

The cemetery's not far away from their last resting place,
but now they'll have the honours earned, a headstone and a face.
A place where families can come and mourn. Honour their dead.
A place of quiet tranquillity. Flags flying overhead.

The thirtieth of January, year two thousand and ten
The first man will be reburied and more each day until then
they have buried all two fifty souls. Flags flutter overhead
as England, Australia and France pay homage to their dead.

And somewhere there's a Didekoi, a Gypsy lad, a fighting man
Whose final resting place is France. He'll no more see the green land
where he walked the lanes with Plodder, the big sixteen hand Shire.
He'll stay forever at Fromelles. A hero killed under fire.

Maureen Clifford

Freedom

You have the right to complain in vain
They have the right to ignore truth
Such a pain
Dead and dying on the battlefields
Since Adam and Eve
Wars will end only when
Humanity dies.

Freedom.

John McCartney

What Is War?

What is war?
War is hate
A greedy state
Die vegetate
War is care
Share the pain
Protect the lame
Don't die in vain
War is confusion
The enemy who
Friend or foe
He creeps near you
See his eyes
Azure-blue
They die at you
He hits the blue
Trauma for you

Pam Mills

Face the Battle

Neither side would want to fight,
Orders must prevail,
Silent darkness of the night,
Families trust could fail.

A soldier's cry of pain and hate,
Attended sharp with worry,
The battle front is an awaiting fate,
So the front line men should hurry.

War is nothing more than death,
For those who know what's next,
The many others who hold their breath,
Should next time read the text.

But war is such a dangerous place,
That humans dread to see,
If we knew what soldiers face,
I'd be glad that it's not me.

The mounds of dead are motionless,
But all still human in their heart,
All fearless you could say,
But war did surely tear them apart.

The bodies left to rot and decay,
Will forever be unretrieved,
The ones who live, go home they may,
But many families will be aggrieved.

Emily Fullwood

Death Camp

boarding the train
cold, cramped . . .
penetrating fear
ripped your
soul open . . .
you knew the real truth
journey into the
worst hell . . .
a nightmare of
betrayal
work makes you
useful
not free,
always smoke
obscuring the sun
there enclosed by electric wire
screams, hanging
shooting, slow pains
of starvation . . .
you know where
you are going
it isn't death
when your
spirit escapes
when you return
from whence
you came, no,
death as cruel finality
is when others know
(and they did know)
and they do nothing

George Coombs

The Lifeless Sky

I don't want to be a hero for another minute more,
I don't want to be disturbed with every scream and roar,
I don't want another handshake or rapturous applause,
Just hand me over the contract and I'll sign the get-out clause,
I don't want this itchy cape that rides up my bum,
I don't want those clumsy idiots always expecting me to come,
My name's never out of the news, or my photo off the front page,
I don't want the leading role on the world's chaotic stage,
I don't want the power of ten, that's the end of all my stunts,
Just make me like the rest and feel some pain for once,
I've had the best-looking women, the fame and the wealth,
In trying to save the world I've nearly been killed myself,
I don't care for the human race and the planet they thought was flat,
Let the suicidal maniacs hit the ground with a splat,
Their rampaging riots, raging fires and overflowing bins of rot,
The villains that want to conquer can have the whole damn lot,
So stop your bickering and fighting, leave me the hell alone,
I don't want to be disturbed, so leave your message after the tone.

Ian McNamara

A Soldier's Dilemma

They think Daddy's on 'holiday'
Not long will they be apart,
Daddy's away, praying silently for peace,
But hope is still in his heart.

It's a position in which
No man should ever be.
But he's willing to fight for freedom,
In defence of his country.

What if he lives?
His expenditure would have been in vain.
But what if he dies?
He will never see his loved ones again.

What actually is war?
Simply a losing game?
Minority live to bear their scars,
But their lives will never be the same.

Confusion wreaked havoc in his mind,
Was he sent to kill or to die?
An epiphany shot through him like a bullet,
It was time to go over the top and face the sky.

Doom washed over him,
As he stepped into the light.
His men, his friends, his brothers,
Had killed themselves in fight.

His opposites were squatted,
Rifles close to hand,
He waited, heard a shot,
Clutched his heart and fell to the sand.

Laura Bruce

Blood-Red Poppies

Paper poppies filled the palms of children
A flickering light at the centre of each
Each child spoke a name, one of the fallen
Names etched upon the war memorial
Placed their poppy upon the altar table
Until the final name was spoken
Spoken with innocence by a small child
Who gently squeezed her flickering poppy
Onto the table of dancing lights
The light of all those lives lost in battle
A poignant reminder . . . the price of freedom
A boy scout walked forward . . . proud and free
Spoke clearly from memory, word for word
A poem of Flanders fields' blood-red poppies

David M Walford

Kill Or Be Killed

I'm sitting surrounded by gunfire and mud having a rest
till it's my turn to run and cross over the wire to kill or be killed
I know I am fighting for freedom for all and pray I
can help bring this about my life is worth nothing
when you see all the pain as young men lie dying
and screaming for help but we cannot reach them
so we sit helplessly by and listen to their prayers as they slowly die
I'd change the world if I had a chance and war would
be over and peace would remain but I hear the whistle
it's my turn to go into the fight and give all of my
strength so if you should know me say a prayer for me
and all of the young men who are all around.

Ann Morgan

Blood-Red Of Man

I am a poppy of Man,
Blood-red in tone,
A petal of Flanders,
Oh how I've grown!

From blood of man
I raised my head,
A Remembrance of heroes
Each one dead.

I am the memory of a soldier
Who went through hell,
I grow in the fields
Where once men fell.

Remember them all
When in the fields I dance,
Blood-red of man
Give me a glance.

Tell of their story
When you see me bloom,
Their spirit will be lifted,
Be not gloom.

I thrive on the land
Where your brothers lie,
Now take your poppy
And wear with pride.

I am a symbol of freedom
That our soldiers gave,
Their memory I carry
They fought so brave.

Be proud to wear me
Upon your chest,
They fought for you
Now they rest.

Dianne Audrey Daniels

My Brave Soldier

To my soldier of past wars
I am still very proud of you
Remembering the fox holes
And loneliness you knew

For months out in the jungle
In the desert or on the battlefield
Injured yourself and watching
As your friends were killed

You said, 'Just serving the nation,
My duty is for the country'
You're back without a great reception
Of ribbons on the trees

But this wife loves you
And remembers with regret
You gave it all for this country
But are not acknowledged yet

A few medals, some group photos
But for you, it was the way to go
Now older and still proud to be British
I admire and love you so

Victorine Lejeune Stubbs

Peace Vs Pride

An economic foundation based on a web of lies,
An international allegiance to strengthen ties,
A hidden agenda behind a façade to aid,
The web of deception has very carefully been laid,

A kingdom built on tears,
People oppressed by their fears,
Patriotism used as propaganda,
Officials comfortably seated on the veranda,

A grave injustice which is branded as 'fate'
Where innocents are used as bait,
So-called 'success' is achieved but at what cost?
The thousands of innocent lives that have been lost,

A system that measures tragedies in profit and loss,
The need to be referred to as the 'boss'
A system which reeks of corruption,
End result of which will be total destruction,

A political campaign based on fighting injustice,
Evidence manipulated to show justice,
A mother waits for a son that will never return,
He is no more the bitter truth she has yet to learn.

The eyes that are all-seeing
The heart that is all-knowing
A prayer that sends the sky shaking,
Victory is ours for the taking.

Farah Ali

Talk Is Cheap

Politicians talk the talk,
Do TV interviews and walk the walk,
Tell us what's wrong and right,
Then stay home safe, sending others to fight the fight,
Young men leaving their children, their wife,
Servicemen and women prepared to sacrifice their life,

Politicians must realise war is not a game,
It tears families apart, their lives will never be the same,
We civilians admire our veterans, of that there is no doubt,
They experience things so dreadful, which they never talk about.
So politicians, when you talk the talk and walk the walk
Be sure your decisions are right,
Mostly consider the brave people that you send to fight your fight.

Maureen Arnold

Shot At Dawn

Why did you wait for the day to break
For God's light to fill the sky
Before you placed the blindfold on his head
And ordered him to die?

Did you witness the sheer terror
In the eyes of my only son?
Did you listen to his heartbeat
As you loaded up that gun?

His mind was paralysed by fear
With images he could not bear
Too terrified to shed a tear
No emotion left to care

A war that ripped his soul apart
And made his spirit flee
Why Lord did he run the other way
Instead of back to me?

This would certainly not have been
The path of life that he would choose
And I pray to God that no son of yours
Will ever walk in his shoes

Elizabeth Slater Hale

Why War?

Under attack
Bullets flying
Breath coming in uneven gasps
Nations embroiled
In war and strife
Peace is answer
Not bomb or blast
Lives are lost
And torn apart
Because nations can't get on
What the hell are we doing?
Where did we go wrong?
A silence that's so quiet
It's deafening
Descends
It's almost eerie to the ears
Pressures of war are heightening
Going on for years and years.

Donna Louise Salisbury

The Poster

They went because it said they should
No guarantees of return, was understood
Your country needs you, the message it gave
All who signed up, were so very brave.

They marched together, brothers in arms
They left behind their factories and farms
They heard those speeches, filled with hate
By a Nazi leader, who sought to dictate.

Interred in prison camps, treated like slaves
Those names shine on in quiet graves
Lord Kitchener's poster gave men inspiration
To pick up weapons and fight for their nation.

They faced their foes in no-man's-land
With rifles, pistols, grenades in hand
They had a camaraderie, hard to be broken
Of those who perished, kind words are spoken.

As the mists of battle, slowly cleared
More fallen soldiers then appeared
Eyes were fixed upon approaching figures
With nervous fingers upon their triggers.

Exploding shells whistled in their ears
Seeing dead comrades produced many tears
Fighting an enemy who were kith and kin
Raising a rifle, committing the greatest sin.

They showed their backbone, showed their spine
The dreaded swastika, they hated the sign
That negative thought known as hate
These brave men sought to disintegrate.

Close your eyes, say a prayer for men with courage so very rare
Let a tear fall from your eyes, as poppies descend from the sky.

Brian Ballard

The Evacuee

During the war I was an evacuee
I was still a schoolgirl then you see
I visited Suffolk, Yorkshire too
Berkshire, Cornwall and the sea was so blue

In Suffolk we picked pounds of sloes
For wine so all could drown their woes
But Cornwall was my favourite place
That lovely sand and sea and space

Apart from school, what did we do
To help our country to get through?
We worked with potatoes and that was tough
As thistles could be very rough

But on the cliffs the locals said, 'No
You'll never get potatoes to grow
Nothing will grow in that poor soil'
We proved them wrong after much hard toil

At first we planted them in rows
And then we worked very hard with hoes
To dig out all the weeds that grew
Although I'm sure we left a few

How thankfully we harvested our crops
We really thought we were the tops
Now if you don't believe it's true
I have a photo I could show you

My friends and I in '41
Working in Cornwall
And spuds by the ton!

Sheila Gymer

Their Soldier Son

She remembered so well, this sweet child, when young,
Playing soldiers with jeeps, tanks and two fingers gun,
He joined the army cadets, his pride and joy of every occasion,
this army-mad boy.
Here we are now, on leave and fit, muscular, tall, packing his kit.
Been here and there including Iraq, now to Afghanistan, he looked forward to that.
She did not say what was in her heart but dreaded the time he had to depart.
She and her husband always knew this is all their son wanted to do.
Now came time to say goodbye, she thought he must not see his mother cry.
Good luck, write soon may God be your guide, they kissed and hugged, her
heart breaking inside.
He smiled as he swaggered down the path and blew a kiss to all,
Ready and fit with a bag full of kit, to answer the Regiment's call.
It was a pleasant warm summer day, birds and bees in the garden at play,
An army officer came up the path, they wondered the reason he came,
There was only one, her heart ran cold, when he asked to confirm their name.
He told them their son had lost his life in a battle of the Taliban's strife.
A model son and they loved him so much, there was no one they could blame,
They clung to each other in private grief and prayed it would not be in vain.

Patricia Evans

Battle Of The Somme

Battle of the Somme, Battle of the Somme
Soldiers marching to the beat of the drum
Boots squelch in mud as onwards they go
Facing their enemy - facing their foe

Young soldiers yearning for home
Battle of the Somme, Battle of the Somme
Tired and weary, lungs filled with mustard gas
War raging on until it reaches an impasse

Broken limbs and torsos flying in the air
Sights too dreadful for anyone to bear
Battle of the Somme, Battle of the Somme
Lives have ended while the drum beats on

The drums beat on my boys, the drums beat on
The battle-weary soldier takes up his gun
While more soldiers are blown to kingdom come
Battle of the Somme, Battle of the Somme

Elizabeth Ann Farrelly

Brothers At War
(Remembrance)

As the rain trickles down the windowpane . . .
My tears mimic the same . . . coursing slowly down my face . . .
As my heart is in a very sad place.

The stereo is loud . . .
The song playing, within my heart hits a chord,
Oh! Why have you taken my Son from me dear Lord?

He went to fight in a foreign country, terrible sights and war to face,
To a country that's been at war for centuries . . .
To do with land, religion and race.

For him, not just a job of nine to five . . .
He joined up to travel, experience and feel alive.
A cause, a pride, of courage, try to change the future for this
country's child . . .
To banish living amongst fear, death, to help them, instead, thrive.

Yes, I know dear Lord . . . that I should be proud . . .
Of him, and so many other mothers' sons . . .
We laugh at them when young, running round playing soldiers with toy guns,
Not realising one day, that a real one will take him away.

The news of his death, the cries of me his mother weeping, could be
heard aloud,
Standing at the airport, awaiting the arrival of his coffin, flying
him home,
As on contact with terra firma, it's covered with a Union Jack shroud
And though my heart is bleeding, I can't help be proud.

Buried with honours, now two months or more, I try to move on,
But I can't mask my anger and the torturous hurt . . .
Like now, as I sit and hug his old rugby shirt . . .
And ask dear God, how many of our sons will we have to bury
under the dirt . . . ?

Pray, before this war and other horrors can end . . .
Please, all your love and prayers send . . .
To all the brave men and women, brothers on all sides,
in God's law . . .
That fight today and who've gone before . . .
Who fight for the cause . . .
As Man has many flaws . . .
And is the instigator of many centuries of bloody wars.

So pray with me then, for these battles to cease . . .
And pray for a world instead of love, charity and peace.

Deborah Harvey

Warfare

Satan is always ready to whisper
Just when your mind is tired
He knows when you are weak
Despondent at the latest bad news
He waits for when you're downcast
To shoot his arrows home
Then he has you captive
'What's the use?' you say
There is no purpose in living now
Yet the pain is nothing new
We have been through it all before
Be aware, don't blame yourself
You know what is behind it
Good and evil in conflict again
The battle continues . . .

May God give us the victory

Irene Grant

Soldier Soul

'Purvey me your soul,' the devil cried
To a war-torn and downtrodden warrior,
'We'll descend through the Earth,
An insidious place,
Much deeper than any old collier.'

Looked up from the ground,
The young soldier did,
Looked him firm and square in the eye,
'I've done no wrong,
Just done as I'm told
And I'll not visit you and fry.'

The Devil looked back,
A pervasive glance,
Said, 'You'll come with me it's your time.'
'We'll plunge to the core,
To my sizzling lounge
And there you'll pay for your crime.'

A cool, subtle retort,
Came from the young man,
'I'm not the reason you came.'
'In a place just like this,
Ubiquitous, you are
And you're looking for someone to blame.'

'Blame?' he replied,
'No not on your life,
I'm looking for someone to praise.'
'He's an equal to me,
As black as can be,
A salute and a glass we'll raise.'

'Whoever he is,
He's done a good job,
Of embroiling himself in this war.'
'With reasons that are,
So way above me,
So why? Even I'm not sure.'

The soldier rang back,
'No neither am I,
I was sent here, my job is to fight,
I do as I'm told,
Day in and day out,
I don't reason what's wrong and what's right.'

'Well you're not the one
I'm looking for.'
The riposte made the soldier relax,
'There are much bigger fish
Out there to get snagged,
In the boiling pot, now that's Iraq.'

'So what is your name?'
the Devil asked boy,
'It's George, I'm a patron saint,
And the reason I'm here,
Is to defend against you,
The soldiers whose names that you taint.'

The Devil's jaw dropped,
An exchange then ensured,
A battle of pure good against pure evil.
With no weapons drawn,
Just colloquy and chat,
Between George and a fed-up old Devil.

When they came to the end,
A decision was made,
About who would make Hell's extradition?
Not the soldiers at all,
Though they fight and they fall,
It must be a war monger, politician

Mark Christmas

We Always Remember

Did they know I was there?
For they had my name and number.
Felt like I was just one of the crowd,
But teamwork we will always remember.

Our laughs and fun were short-lived,
For silence and then the roar of battle.
Sick with blood, sweat and death,
Emotionally ripped to bits, hard to tackle!

Marching on for victory and peace,
A destiny hard to imagine exists.
For the stench of gunfire and smoke,
Follows like ghosts whirling in an ugly mist!

Were we forgotten, the lucky ones,
The bullets missed so marched home.
In the sunshine are they really gone?
Quiet, but then one hears the drone.

Ann Beard

Photograph Of A Young Man

Imagine the man from the folded photograph
Yellowed by time, creased inside a wallet pocket,
Squatting amongst the dead and dying
In the thick mud of a trench, clutching on
To the silent rifle with his numb hands
Surrounded by a fog of smoke
And the charred, broken fragments of the trees,
Waiting on a whistle.
Now look at the photograph again
And try to forget.

Siegfried Baber

World War One

Sometimes I simply sit and ponder,
While gazing out on our garden green;
Had I lived at the time I wonder,
What would my fate in the war have been?

A call-up letter through our front door;
My destiny changed by written word:
Perhaps with a baby in the pram
And family left so ill-prepared!

Would I have joined in the revelry?
With friends so willing to do or die;
Then seeing them show such bravery
But witness too, many brave men cry!

Could I have survived the stinking mud?
With shattered bodies scattered around;
Putrefying in a sea of blood
And me pinned down on the spattered ground!

Should I have mingled my fear with rage?
At human folly of wasting life;
Bad memories left not to assuage
And feel contempt for the futile strife!

Yet evil forces when they conspire
To threaten our cherished freedom's way,
Leave little choice but to raise such ire
And defiant, risk the deadly fray.

Many with valour did freedom serve,
Who died or endured - I know not how!
But lasting gratitude they deserve
For I can ponder in freedom now.

Bill Newham

They Look So Young

A veteran now you feel your age
You watch the men and women on parade
They look so young almost childlike
Yet they carry death before them.
They are your shield and protector
Will beat repel the savage beast
That threatens freedom's liberty
That beast you fought in bloody combat
Left you with your fallen comrades
Cradled dying in blood-soaked arms
Their childlike youth destroyed and lost
Amongst the thunder of the night.
Later in the stillness . . . silence
You brought back your fallen comrades
Draped them in a flag of honour
Knowing your innocence and youth
Were lost forever . . . lost in thunder.

D M Walford

Charge Again

Swords clash on the ground
They thrust with the point
Into the joint
Howls and screams
All abound
Blood falls on the ground
In this hell all around
Warriors charge on horseback too
With lances to run through
They will charge
Again and again
So much agony
So much pain
As cannons crack out again
Where blood runs in the rain
Arrows strike and kill many in flight
On this blooded night

Gordon Forbes

Warhorse

Drawing your gaze a huge horse
With across his forehead a brave white
Blaze, echoed on his nose and
On his four fetlocks a mighty pair of hocks.
Capable of carrying enormous weight,
Powerful and not clumsy his gait.
This is the fabled warhorse, forced to
Carry its medieval cross.
In fact, a knight in full armour, bearing
Sword and lance, under grim fiery conditions
Having to gallop through enemy positions,
Undertaken in the best war traditions.
Without them there would have been no
King Arthur and his trusty knights.
Neither Black Knight, nor White Knight
Riding forth to fight, sworn to maintain
Every loyal citizen's right, contesting evil
Protecting each child and maid crying out
For aid. Each rider honing his skill in the
Tilt Yard, entering the lists to fight to the
Death, but occasionally fortune would
Prove an ally, so that one defeated would be
Spared, then the victor would sheath his sword,
Returning her silk favour
And from his princess collect his reward,
A passionate hug and a kiss at further courtship
Would labour, culminating in a lifetime of bliss,
Their mating creating much happiness, ever after
To savour; of course, very thankful, to his warhorse.

Graham Watkins

Old Friends

So comfortable together
They now marched side by side,
Though their hides were tough as leather,
They strode along with pride . . .
Their fearsome tusks like scimitars,
Their eyes as dark as night,
With tiny twinkling nestled stars
Inside them, shining bright . . .
Their feet as tough as army boots
Sent trembling through the ground . . .
Like old friends smiling in cahoots,
Just swaggering around . . .
Defiant against any foe!
Just bring it! If you dare!
They'd fight them all, give blow for blow,
As if they didn't care . . .
The other creatures gave them space . . .
Why make the giants mad?
Why anger them, so they give chase . . .
And lose the life you had?
And so, the old friends swaggered by,
Like playground bullies do . . .
Bull elephants! Don't ask them why,
If you know what's good for you . . .

Denis Martindale

Those Millions Left Behind

What of those millions left behind;
Read between the lines!
Whose fathers knew they were so blind;
Thinking things were fine;
I think of those particularly,
The surface barely scratched,
Whose precious sons were sent away,
Their mothers' arms detached;
Who were these ones the records skimp?
Most before my time,
I can't relate - but barely glimpse,
That heinous, wicked crime!

When I think of Kipling's blighted verse;
Hark, the beating drum!
He, once full - exuberance;
The dark and final sum . . .
And a music hall comedian,
Humour was the rote,
Till his precious son from him was torn,
Keep on! He was smote;
And other's sons they felt they should,
Ships of dubious plate,
Submarine the aim was good,
Quickly sealed their fate;

And recently (one man knows why)
Red-caps honour signed;
Bereft of weapons - justify;
By some lunatic confined;
The millions more that war inflicts,
Limiting the whole,
Grieving fathers - truth restricts,
A mother's stricken soul;
Upon their hands - upon their cloth,
Blood upon their clout,
To feed his belly - Moloch's wrath,
Religion's haughty pouch . . .

And millions more I have to say;
Children's bodies smashed;
Or lingered till they went away;
Their hopes so cruelly dashed;
While politicians smoothly glib,
And justify their stance,
And dig their cronies in the ribs,
Blood guilt, heaven's glance!
For they did croak with smooth cliché,
Weapons should release,
'This war provoke - no other way,
But guard the future peace'

And what of these leaders who stay behind,
Who beggar our belief;
And look for profits - 'Keep them blind . . .
Give them no relief!'
Though voices raised in sanity,
(Try their conscience mar)
Speak against their vanity . . .
'Damn their cries for war!'
What of those millions left behind,
Parents left to grieve,
Each death a blueprint in God's mind,
This I do believe . . .

Tom Ritchie

Emblems And Symbols/ Poppies And War

It is a human thing, this naming and claiming of symbols,
As Adam did, walking in Eden when all was new;
Seeing the majestic oak as strong, the shy fox as sly,
And the maligned snake cursed for all time.
Ancient caves are drawn with the animals of the hunt,
In the colours of soil and blood, and buffalo, deer and men
Jostle the walls, glow and leap in our flickering light.
Long before the Chinese took the lotus as symbol
For the humble peasant, seeing it push from the mud,
Strong and constant, it bloomed of its own accord,
Cast off petals in the wind, filled the pod with tough seeds,
Falling and growing again. It stands aloof and beautiful
Adorning temple pools, among the great leaf discs,
Non-aligned and remote, but still we grasp the symbol,
Take it for Buddha, for humanity, for hotel logos;
And so it is with the poppy, which is just a weed that springs
On fallow fields. It cannot help being scarlet as blood,
Blood that spilled on battlefields. The poppy blooms
In bewitching scarlet to charm the butterfly, that hippy thing,
That twitches in tattoos on ageing skin, and so it goes . . .

Liz Davies

Vigil Of A Wounded Soldier

Sitting silent there
She a vigil kept.
In empty tears
Her kind heart wept
With sobbing prayers
She guards my soul
Her kind loving voice
My heart console.

Then joins her hands,
And kneels to pray
Just as she does
Each and every day.
Then our loving eyes
Weep, turn and meet
In everlasting joy
At each heartbeat.

My time on earth,
Now is over, past,
But her love
Will forever last
I touch her hand
I've no more fears.
The holy angel
Of the Lord appears.

Anthony Page

Falklands War Memories

Dead comrades

Black bodies bubble,
Silently charred,
In death's dark doorways.

Drowning.

The bell tolls.

Absolution.

Spasms of facial contortion,
Through which they no longer smile.

Under fire,
Under siege.

Screams,
Shattered minds,
All manner of broken dreams.

Unspun,
In destiny's web.

Undone,
In time.

Made to die.

Congealed,
Without hope,
Unchanged by moulding hands,
Unsurpassed in illness,
Undreamt.

Picture a thread through a needle,
The needle in your life,
Poking you,
Mocking your heart,

Killing you.

It sees beyond the façade,
Through which you try to smile.

Post-traumatic stress disorder

The demons in the dream scream,
Flickering as flames in a grate,
Whirling flitting incandescence,
Rising upwards,
Born upwards,
In an orange tinted half light,
Floating upwards,
Born upwards,
Spiralling,
Spinning,
Taunting you they float,
Haunting,
Grinning.

A bed in the middle of a floor,
A room with no walls,
Windows with cracked panes,
Shattered shards cut you,
Pierce your soul,
Your spirit hidden from you,
You lie alone,
Your head in your hands,
Nail-biting,
Perpetual grimness.

And all there is,
A vision,
Through mists and rain,
Of words swirling,
Of poetry peeping through keyholes,
When you're sleeping,
Of delightful escapism and happy moments,
They taunt you,
And are gone,
Even before hands can grasp them.

Pin your thoughts to the ground,
Hang your head alone,
There's no speaking when you drown.

Michael A Wride

For the Government's Problems

For the government's problems
our good men die.
For the government's problems
young children cry.
For the government's problems
our nights are blacked out.
For the government's problems
there's no benefit of a doubt.
It's not our fault;
we are sent to fight.
It's not our fault
that life's no delight.
It's not our fault
that we have no choice.
It's not our fault -
we can't use our voice.
For the government's problems
we're not allowed to forgive.
For the government's problems
we can't freely live.
For the government's problems
hardship's our life.
For the government's problems
we live with trouble and strife.

Maria Dixon

Beauty In Terror

As a very young child
Growing up during a war
It's amazing thinking back
At some wonders that I saw
Picking blackberries one afternoon
Quite a way from home
It was frightening to hear
A dreaded noise, aeroplane drones
Diving under the gorse bushes
Not thinking of the thorns
Just wanting Mum and the shelter
But alone and forlorn
The planes were friend and foe
Ducking and diving they spat at each other
I watched at all so I should know
The vapour trails were beautiful
Leaving a pattern in the sky
When suddenly the foe turned tail
Short of fuel it was time for goodbye
Thinking back I hope the boys
That piloted the planes
Arrived home safely to their loved ones
Both of them the same

Daphne Fryer

Poppies

Poppy petals fluttering down
Like a bright red eiderdown,
In contrast with the stark white stones
On the graves of soldiers' bones.
Boys and men who went to fight the foe
To protect their country that they loved so,
The bugler played his lively song
'Take the King's shilling lads, come along.
Join the army and see the world
See bloody battles come unfurled'
Off they went to serve and fight
Little did they realise the enemy's might.
Lived in filthy, mud-filled trenches
'Sit on your arses, we don't have benches,
Keep your heads down until you're told
Then up and over lads, brave and bold'
Over they went into fields of mud
Splattered with bodies, red with blood,
Thousands and thousands every day
Died in those fields so far away.
Every minute men were dying
Leaving families grieving, crying,
Young men taken in the prime of life
Never again to see mother or wife.
Nor would they see a sunny sky
Birds and bees come flying by,
There they lie in that far-off land
In rows of graves so straight, so grand.
Is this what they came for, so willing?
Was it worth taking that 'King's shilling'?
Those brave men who died so that we
Could live our lives, safe and free.

Dorothy Fuller

To Remain Untouched

Absorption of time
Solitary vision, assumes an enchantment
Yet through the dark, through the light on sepia
Memory is committed
Numbness
Its contours obsessively unfulfilled
Preoccupation assumed
The intimacy distinct to the soul
Vague awareness of the dark and light
Not submissive beyond the dreams
Recurring in the background of consciousness
The eyes receive in dreamless recognition
Though persistence accepts
Through invasion of absorption
The habitation of memory, distinct versions are accumulated
Some proportions are vague in ignorance
Knowledge capacity is preoccupied
Staying unresponsive in shadows of dark and light
Sometimes defining a tangent
A weakness, only prevalent to the inner eyes of the resonance
of harmony
The affirming image positive
The shattered harmony unfocused
In the concentration to remain expressionless
To be untouched by symmetry

Hilary Jean Clark

A Tragic Summer

In Helmand Province - ever mounting
Loss of life - we're steady counting
Grim statistics - hard to swallow
How many deaths will surely follow?

From this mortal world - departing
On a journey - comrades starting
Mates together - none are strangers
No more hidden deadly dangers.

To a hope their loved ones clinging
'We will see them - someday' - bringing
Comfort/joy - all pain releasing
Grief and sorrow - slowly ceasing.

Stephen John Glason

The Fallen

I see through shining leaves the white crosses of the white knights
Their names etched on cold marble
I walk the stone-lined trenches and cannot fail to hear the cries of battle and the
smell of fear
The splash of boots that ran as one towards the tolling of the bell
The men who never saw another summer, cried out their one last prayer before
they fell
Spring still raged across the fields beyond and somewhere the birds still sang
But here there was no paradise - so much of Hell so much of sacrifice
Incessant gunfire and the clagging mud
The desperate cries of men who never would
Hear the wild surf again or see rebirth in nature's greening hand
Who lie in ceremonial display like knights of old, swords laid to rest
Unchallenged occupiers of a foreign land

Margaret Whitehead

The Unknown Soldier

You were the one on the French fields,
You were the one in the Siberian snow,
You were the one 'neath the Polish pall,
Who suffered the terminal blow;
Undiscovered, a leaf to the wind,
Lost to time and circumstance,
A still heart lay,
If to be found by chance.

What worth in the hinge of goodbye,
When he let go of her hand,
When tears spoke through the silence,
Painful parting to understand . . .
That someone may not return,
Least of all be unnamed,
To languish in a muddy morass,
Only by the weather claimed?

You were a father,
You were a mother,
You were a sister,
You were a brother;
We acknowledge in respect,
A man, a woman whom . . .
Is the unknown soldier,
Resting in the tomb.

Andrew Gruberski

The House Of War

Across the world has ever but been
Stood but the house of war
A house that stood on many lands
A house that stood in history's gates

For in it was but an unhappy place
Place of places
Where power was run by people far away
Made of the fortunes
Out of the trade in armaments
That sustain the wealth
Of these people far away
And lets the weapons stand
To wreak havoc on the lives
Of those in the house of war
Lives lived in the gloom of war

War that is but all known
The trials and tribulations of the guns
So many stand but in the light
And speak of times that passed
When peace was but around
But in a wistful light
Now all is but war
War has held all in its firm embrace

While in the other world
Of the house of peace only peace reigns
War reported by the media runs
Never does it disturb the lives of people there
While industries make arms to provide riches and jobs
Built on the misery of the others.

Alasdair Sclater

Fallen Heroes

The endless conflict, the bloody field
A mother's son should never see
And yet their lives forever yield
So others walk this land as free
Gasping for a painful breath
Gaping wounds, limbs scattering
The binding a bright red wet
The bombs a death knell hammering

Faces stare from our screens
Strangers to our minds
Pride exudes from heroic beings
Of terror there are no signs
Now no more, their duty done
Another life snuffed out
Succumbed to a hostile gun
A family left without

Now only mourning has a place
Lives broken forever be
Duty performed with such grace
Such selfless bravery
And left behind lives torn apart
Never to be repaired
It's not the end, it is the start
Just because they dared

Barbara Lambie

In A Room Of A Thousand Faces

In a room of a thousand faces
I feel so lost and lonely
In a room of generated heat
I feel the winter cold

Smile for the sake of it
As it seems that's what I should do
Keeping up my wall of invincibility
While I crumble like Cheshire cheese

My sense of loss compounded
By watching the nightly bulletin
Another name, another mother crying
As she gets the MOD news

Killed serving their country
Be proud, as they were brave
But pride can only stand hand in hand
With anger and resentment for a war that is not ours to fight

As I look at the picture of my girl
I remember her pride on her posting
The day forever in my mind
For a few months later, I cry for the love I've lost

Paul Holt

Poppies

Blooming wild in far-off fields
    A crimson lake of poppies grow,
In homage to the loss of life
    That occurred so long ago.

Flanders field is but one of those
    Battlefields of that great war,
Wounded, limping home to find
    Poverty, hardship, empty store.

My grandfather fell in the Somme
    His widow had four children small,
The poppies blooming in the fields
    Cannot pay this debt at all.

We owe so much to the fallen men
    Their sacrifice was vast,
Poppies every year must show
    Their courage has not passed.

In our hearts the poppies bloom
    Wear them displayed with pride,
Heroes gone, kept evergreen,
    By our respect, deep inside.

Elizabeth Stanley-Mallett

World War One

World War One
A job well done?
Or a slaughterhouse of men
The Germanic formation
V the more western nations
So needless, all those lives spent

National prides
Make ready brides
For revenge to have a wedding
And all too soon
There comes high noon
And warwards we were heading

The primary cause
Was simply because
Of Russia's movement for growth
The Triple Alliance
Was formed in defiance
And nations plighted their troth

But the sown seeds
Turned straight into weeds
The Triple Entente was our lot
Opposing sides formed
When the dreaded day dawned
And Austria's archduke was shot

The deed had been done
And the Germans begun
Attacking a neutral at peace
As Belgium's good friend
We replied to defend
And the chaos war was released

Through the mud and the mire
'Neath the downpour of fire
The soldiers fought in their trenches
In rain and in mud
The gunfire shed blood
Against gas, they lacked in defences

In those bitter fought battles
They were slaughtered like cattle
Until that final November
Five million lost
Was the true cost
And that we should always remember

Ray Ryan

The Objective

He holds a gun in his hands,
Ready for the attack,
It maybe his last stand,
There is no turning back.

One of a force,
Striving for peace,
The war will run its course,
The trigger waiting for release.

Together comrades,
Banded forever,
Likened to the Crusades,
Friendships never to sever.

Jonathan Simms

November, November

Shelled buildings stood stark with walls missing,
Sightless windows, and sightless people
Laid lifeless in the dust and rubble,
Fires burning, flaring and hissing.

A home stands ravaged and derelict
Where Granny has died, the falling bombs
Had not stirred any fear in her;
She had lived through another conflict.

But lying there in the muck and slime,
Her thin hand stuck up in defiance,
Clasping her knitting in a fist . . . mark
A spirit unbroken in wartime.

A child stands staring and tears come
For Granny, for Dad away at war,
And for himself the life he had known,
For all is lost in his broken home.

Through many towns and cities this cry
Rises and echoes from many mouths,
A heartfelt loss of precious people
And the lonely wind whimpers and sighs.

And as one year slides to another
People rise again and build their lives,
A blood-red poppy is worn with pride
In mem'ry of fathers and brothers.

Gwendoline Douglas

Afghanistan, Taking On The Taliban

O brave warriors of Camp Bastion,
The conflict in Afghanistan,
A brutal unforgiving war,
Against the cruel Taliban,

Soldiers on foot underneath desert skies,
Drones, helicopters and transports on patrol,
The darkness on a moonless night,
Coalition air-strikes, and war medics,

Clearing operations whilst sweeping for mines,
Brave men and women in armoured vehicles,
Night vision binoculars, rifles and mortar shells,
With heavy machine-gun fire,

The thud of artillery shells exploding,
Running the gauntlet in large convoys,
Military personal ambushed by a roadside bomb,
Detonations and shrapnel litter the desert ahead,

Improvised explosive devices hidden in cotton fields,
That maim and kill, that leave only the dead,
Dying for a cause, the cruel Taliban,
Insurgents and bomb-makers the world does dread,

Helmand Province, nerves of steel to walk that lonely mile,
Civilians blown to bits, blown apart amongst poppy fields of red,
An unforgiving war of casualties and children,
Across this arid land, the walking wounded and the dead,

Fanatical extremists, the Taliban on the run,
With battle-weary men, as a hidden sniper fires,
With bombardments and surprise attacks,
This the horrendous nature of war,

An unstoppable war, so vile is war,
Went a platoon of a hundred me.

James Stephen Cameron

Through Wartime Fears

Being the granddaughter of a soldier
Face up to many things every day,
My dad's father was in Africa,
When the Boer War had its day.
The old photograph has part of the family showing,
My dad, a little boy then, more children to come,
Making it a family of ten.
Later on, uncles became soldiers, girls as nurses
Serving their part
In the 1914-18 war and over.
Then their youngsters of the family
Did their duties in 1939-45.
Being too young to take part
Then being only ten,
I did my best, helping raise money, being in concerts
There was always a 'War Weapons' week,
Money raised was the target
Everyone took part.
Seemed like there was a new song came out every week
Pianist had her work cut out,
As the popular one of the moment
Had to be played and sung
All done with spirit, making things hum.
Lots of mothers like mine, knitted for the forces,
Winter weather not kind.
We had school gardens which were turned to veg,
My friend Gwen and I, complimented on by MOF for our vegetation.
We had our own little plot you see, no intervention.
My dad, as many others, made us bikes from spare parts,
We got around quite well on them
Sometimes pedalling away to the council offices,
Six miles away after school time to get the ration books,
Duly made out to my aunt, expecting her boys,
And my friend Mary, for her brother,
Evacuated with his school of boys.
Another chore we had to do was picking potatoes at Hall Farm.
Nights of bombing to contend with as well.

No sooner had our bombers gone out,
German bombers would whine in, like hell.
Following river and railway lines,
Bombing many places, which were in their sights
Sometimes dropping bombs,
To lighten their load.
Hitting a farmhouse with a direct hit
Killing two people inside who had come away
Each night from their hometown,
To avoid such a night as this.
War will never be the same again,
Am thinking with atomic gloom,
We surely must avoid this cloud,
Which must not be our doom.
I think of our boys in Iraq and Afghanistan
And pray they soon come home.
Seems like a pointless war to me.
I heard the heavy planes go out,
Which filled my heart with fear.
From a nearby airfield here.
The practice flights had been done,
Newspapers made it clear,
There would now be soldiers on board.
Within this flight so near.
My heart was with them as they flew away.
Hoping they will be back soon,
Is my wish every day.

Mabel Deb Moore

He Set Us Free

Thousands of people all over the world
Stand in silence in remembrance of when
Courageous soldiers fell in the wars
The sailors, marines and airmen
To remember those who gave their lives
For their country is noble indeed
Yet it cannot compare to the privilege we have
In partaking at the Lord's table we feed
Celebrating communion, obeying Christ's command
Each time we remember His death, we see
That He sacrificed His life for us
Forgiving our sin He set us free

Catherine M Armstrong

More Death

Daily read of loss, hear names listed on the radio,
Someone's child, husband or lover's lease on life's been let go.
Futility of war not been better demonstrated,
Folk throw wakes for lost loved ones, lives to be celebrated.

When will day come that wars end, innocents killed, awful plight,
Death toll's mounting with no obvious surrender in sight.
Our inclusion in some wars is difficult to understand,
Perhaps people could see if invasion was of own land.

Maybe pull out of war zone, let natives manage alone,
Then let our numerous troops to make the long journey home.
It's certainly a thought which could possibly be pursued,
Another death is announced which makes this mother subdued.

Susan Mullinger

Concentration Camps

Faces were sunken as if into the skull
Heartstrings ached, tugged with a pull
Bodies were lying everywhere around
Silence was deafening, hardly a sound

Many asked for food we'd none to give
Surviving only through sheer will to live
The stench of carrion burned at my nose
Some walked about as if the dead arose

Imagine the worst nightmare ever seen
Horrific sights turning stomachs green
Zombies, the dead, walking right there
Pitiful looks of such torturous despair

We were quite lean fed and watered
Walking amidst near dead or slaughtered
As long as I live this will ever haunt me
Every day passing clear in mind to see

The pains of world war, the true evil of Man
Tortured souls endless a woman and man
Only with time would these souls yet tell
The very real truth, their sheer living hell

Christopher Slater

The Colour Of War

The colour of war for me is red
Remembering the past war heroes dead
It does not matter who, why and when.
Especially when history repeats itself again.
There was red blood on the beaches.
The effects all over the world, war reaches.

Planes, ships and trains, vehicles of the past.
Used to transport the weapons of destruction,
The loss of life was vast.
Men and boys to fight abroad and at home.
Their women carried the land quite often left alone.
The telegrams came bordered in black
Told them of red bloodshed, their men did not come back.

So what has changed? Not too much.
Modern technology now shows us as such.
The atrocities happening all over the world
Young men blown up, the Red Cross flag unfurled.
Today I saw a veteran cry, he was lucky he did not die.
His story was of war in Palestine in defence of two sides of the Jordan.

The bravery of his friends, his memories are golden
The blood shed was red, to them we are beholden
Modern day war is just as intense.
In adverse ways it makes no sense
The poppy flower is as red as their blood
Past, present or future sadly war is never good.

Whatever the outcome, wars leave a terrifying mark
Of leaving the grieving asking why in the dark

Ellen Spiring

War Memorial

Within his mind, engrossed and wrapped,
Fixating images, locked in and trapped.
That child, blown away, clutching grenades
The picture keeps coming, never fades

Pregnant woman, burst belly, hugging foetus,
Staring Heavenwards, praying, but hopeless
Suicide bomber, brainwashed, devoid of wits,
Covered in blood and guts and body bits.

Wounded soldier tries to stand on legless torso,
Trauma infiltrates one's brains, but more so.
The dreams still there, but fades away.
Fighting for one's life, hopefully peace some day.

This hero, this warrior, this fighting man
Is on his way back to Afghanistan
To free that country from the Taliban,
Please, please support him all you can.

Whilst from the comfort of your home
Your thoughts of him in combat zone
Deserving of a poppy, which is due
In recognition from me and you.

Ian Tomlinson

A Moment In Harm's Way

The sounds, the smells are all different
It's far from the world that I knew here
The sound of crying, despair, pain
Always within the cold icy grip of fear

Shouting, orders that could spell my last
The sound of boots grinding the dirt
A battalion goes running past
No time to think, it all goes far too fast
A noise, an explosion, it all runs in slow motion

I can't hear what he's saying
Instinct drives me, tells what to do
Running on automatic pilot
It's how we all get through

At night I dream of blood-coloured cold blue steel
I wake disappointed, yes this world I endure is real
Home seems so far away across unfamiliar foreign lands
Where decisions are made about my fate out of my hands

No time for grief, no time for thought
Only fear and guilt offer to keep me company
Only time for thoughts of survival until the end of the day
No time to ponder tomorrow, any future too uncertain for me

Steve Prout

War Games 1939-1945

Black/white board with no shades of grey.
Expendable pawns line up with obscene neatness
And bow before the wishes of their 'back seat' hierarchy.

As battle begins
The pattern begins
To move, change, develop . . .

As pawns are won or lost
As fortunes fluctuate
As knights move forward . . .

Planning/executing
Bluff and counter bluff countered by bluff -
Lines are challenged, crossed, destroyed
Creating a no-man's-land where sides
Become blurred and issues seem devoid
Of substance when measured against the
Heaps of dead.

Who asks now - what price these principles?

And

When the war is over
When grief has touched
Every piece
Of life

No one will know the number lost
No one will have counted.

For as in all games
Only winners count.

Sue Gerrard

The Fallen

Deep down in the earth, the veins of our promises
flowing and pulsing
like the arms of our fathers
our sons, and our brothers.

We, the circle of life,
ever living yet dying
we consume the air of the fallen
and they consume our tears.

And in that we are everlasting
ever breathing and giving
we're raised up as they're falling.

Natalie Williams

War Games

I watch as the children play war games,
They seem not to realise,
That in real wars the dead stay dead,
Because in their world of fun today,
They all get up from the ground again,
Readily and eager to play another game,
The yells and shouts are just pretend,
No mothers will have to weep or cry,
No fathers have to keep a dry eye,
No siblings will have to bid a sad goodbye,
No babies will grow up without a parent,
No child will look at the stars in the night sky,
No visiting the graves of the brave,
For when their games have ended,
Each one returns to their home.

Pauline Uprichard

Colour Of War

The colour of war is red
For every soldier that's bled
And for every soldier that's died
A wife or mother has cried

Everyone hopes it will end
No more soldiers to send
So many soldiers lost
Such a terrible cost

Why are we doing this?
These people hate us
What are we doing there?
Why should we care?

We have to be strong
And admit it was wrong
To send our troops there
We've taken all we can bear

Even if it means a row
Bring our boys back now
It's the right thing to do
And you know it too

Frank Tonner

Our Brave Soldiers

We await the day with open arms
The coming home of dear ones ours.
Out fighting on the enemy lines,
We die for them a thousand times.

We fear to read the Daily Post,
In fear the news we fear the most,
News we pray we shall not learn,
Longing for the day that they return.

The telephone, who can it be?
We die again until we see
Home insurance, double glazing,
How long before we're worried crazy?

Restless nights and tortured dreams,
Eternity this conflict seems,
Brave ones, loved ones doing their bit,
We await the end to all of it.

That special day to quell our fears,
The coming home our loved ones dear.
Returning safely from enemy lines
To we who have died a thousand times.

Waiting helplessly at home
In fear the post and telephone,
In fear the news lest it be bad,
Each casualty, some special lad.

To those alas who lose their lives,
For their grieving parents and widowed wives,
In verse we honour their soldier men,
Brave in conflict all of them.

Peter Terence Ridgway

A Taste Of War

It was Grandma who spoke of the war
And I listened
As she did her delicious ravioli on a huge table
She used to say it could save lives from bombs and shrapnel
Little could I realise then
The force of a bomb exploding
But Grandma was sure of this
Though she also said she and Mother and all
Rushed to the shelters dug out by the men in the middle of the street
Of hard rock they were made
That no German bomb could reach
And as her stories of the war were said
Of how many bombers came to lay their bombs on the
Maltese heads
Of how Italian pilots released their load and fled
And how German stukas dived with their nose pointed down ahead
Shattering houses and sowing dead
And how one ship limping to port saved the island from instant dread
That the day marked a feast for all that were left
Until the day the island received The Cross for the bravery of her men and women
Who fought and died for their loved ones and the freedom of the world
I too got to know something of the war
Where my pa and ma had also met and loved
But how could I really feel what these people had to go through
for me to be born alive? - I owe it to them!

Cornelius John Mulvaney

Bigotry And War (Cause And Effect)

What is the colour of bigotry?
What shape's prejudice?
How can you draw race hatred?
What sort of task is this?
To draw an accurate picture,
You need such questions answered:
If you don't know what one looks like,
How d'you draw an ignorant b******?

What is the colour of war?
What causes confrontation?
When racial hatred's to the fore,
It leads to conflagration:
What makes one faction feel
That another is inferior?
If evil thoughts are given reign,
Clear vision just gets blearier.

After wars are finished,
Nobody ever wins,
Participants all are losers,
So who atones their sins?
The casualties aren't all soldiers,
Their families are bereft,
War's not about those who are right,
It's about those who are left!

Mick Nash

The Summer the Cicadas Didn't Sing

The summer the cicadas didn't sing

A darkness hung over the world
One powerful leader insisted on a war
Only he and his advisors believed in

The summer the cicadas didn't sing

Some countries found the courage
To defy the great military power
And fell victim to its verbal artillery fire

The summer the cicadas didn't sing

Old soldiers who had witnessed
Previous wars' horrors and still suffering
From the effects added their voices of dissent

The summer the cicadas didn't singularly

The people of the world marched through streets
In numbers never before seen, their
Melancholy voices raised in universal protest

The summer the cicadas didn't sing

The citizens' feelings were totally ignored
And they felt a powerlessness they'd
Never felt or experienced before

The summer the cicadas didn't sing

Everyone held their breath and waited

Gaelynne Pound

The Question

Poppies shining red against the snow-white cross
A stark reminder here of lives lost long ago
So many names forgotten in the mists of time
And battles too that caused such grief and woe.

Just watch awhile and you will surely see
A little lady, bent and frail with age
Walk to the cross and bow her head in prayer
In doing so she turns another page.

A silver teardrop glistens in her eye
As she remembers from long years ago
A single rose she lays upon the cross
And to her God, she simply whispers, 'Why?'

Barbara Dunning

Peace For The Future

Peace is something - has to be earned
It trickles through the universe
But can slip through our numbed fingers
Everyone must work hard for it
Nothing is ever easy
In life - nothing ever is
A steep mountain is hard to climb
One's limbs and sinews hurt and pain
It sometimes seems things take so long
One pulls one's hair in frustration
All around's the slam of bad times
The claps of thunder from dark minds
I nearly gave up my pining
Cried into my hands quite hopeless
But then my dreams brought me back here
I won't be held back - peace must win

Muhammad Khurram Salim

Soldiers Valiantly Marching On!

Valiantly we shall march on,
through the battle and fight
guide us O mighty Lord upon high
and protect us with Your light.

Soldiers marching onwards to fight!
For strong in heart and soul are we,
courageous then and filled with faith
so that the nations can be free.

The guns may blast through the skies,
but we stand tall and never fear!
For victory is always on the horizon
Our Lord almighty is so very near

Many are the dead and the fallen,
our very comrades and close friends
yet amidst the confusion we shall wipe away our tears
and march on, march on till the very end!

To serve our Queen and country so faithfully,
each soldier called to serve by name
and yet we ourselves are not the heroes,
but through the bloodshed we'd do it all again.

Soldiers marching on with heads held high,
with a fighting spirit flowing through out hearts
for we all would welcome peace and freedom to come,
knowing that our Lord will never depart!

Simon Foderingham

The Red Cabaret

How far to the end of the red cabaret?
Bloodshed is my memory.

Pushing deals, the followed news,
Three denials before it's true.
Madmen moved to prophecy
Liars believing all they say.

A woman, rich with Italian coffee,
Out of the west she gave me a taste
Of the old ways. She said softly
Under the huge heave of her breath
'Nothing but the truth was best.'

She had the wisdom of mothers
Who saw their children suffer.
Who believed in a new day.
Knew the link of pain and memory.

Maybe I am cursed too,
Beneath this twilight moon
I have prayed to your idols
I paid my dues.

Or, just blessed all too much.
A pure white zero
Rolled through my head
Like a touch and stroke of luck.

I'm on my feet
In the gunned-down streets.
Pounding black boots
Are running rampage.

This world seems much more
Than any human age can take.
No human thing can feed
Its soul on a feast of nothing.

The axe held high
Is in silhouette against the sky
Blood is back on the agenda.

I dream of the flesh of the Eucharist
A pure white zero
And our bloodstained souls.

John Harkin

Reflect On War

I once had the chance
To visit the battlefields of France
I walked along the shore at low tide
On the very spot our gallant soldiers fought and died
Leaving their bases in the United Kingdom
Over rough seas to fight for our freedom
I walked over sand which soaked up spilled blood
They advanced into France like an incoming flood
Their exploits are still strong in the locals' minds
Knowing our troops had left their loved ones behind
The price for their victory can be seen in the ground
Where row upon row of white crosses can be found
The war graves are well tended, peaceful and serene
The prime of our youth now lie under that grass so green
You cannot but leave but with a tear in your eye
While the birds still sing happily in the sky
I sadly left with one thought going on in my mind
War solves nothing or are all statesmen totally blind?

Leonard Butler

D - Day

The boy lay trembling on the sand, crying for his mother,
Rigid with fear, not daring to move, scanning the beach for cover.
Just seventeen; too young to die - too young to be a soldier;
He'd joined the army under-age; he'd told them he was older,
And now he wished with all his heart he hadn't been so eager
To put his life upon the line for rewards so scant and meagre.
But - too late now to have regrets - it wouldn't do at all
To wallow in self-pity as he watched his comrades fall.
So he tried to blank his mind to the terrifying sound
Of screams from wounded men and shells exploding all around.
And, with an inner strength he didn't know he had,
He surged forward with his regiment, this young, courageous lad.
And, against all odds, this boy survived to fight another day,
And came back home to Blighty, having been some years away.
And, do I swell with pride to tell this tale? Yes - rather!
Because, my friend, I'm proud to say that boy became my father.

Heather Pickering

Len

In the warm cosy snug of our old village pub
Len downs a pint and whisky galore
And tells his adventures that thrill to the core.
How he rode a white camel 'cross Arabian sands
The photo clutched proudly in gnarled old hands

Len is a hero of village folklore.
With Sterling's mob he went to war
And fought with the best so we might be free
To live in peace and harmony.
But Len paid a price that is awful to watch,
Which is why he keeps drinking those bottles of scotch

Ben Corde

The Cult Of The Hero

'Eroes? Ha! You don't know the 'arf of it!
Sittin' at 'ome, thinkin' war's a game!
Most of us wouldn't be 'ere, we wasn't conned!
'By Christmas' is getting' lame . . .

'Don't' want t'lose you - we think you ought t'go?'
Huh! You want this hell f'your son?
Think the Fritz's are runnin' scared?
Or the enemy's the side we're not on?

P'rhaps y' mean the officers?
Them what carry little while we trudge,
What live in dugouts; wi' proper food an' roofs?
We sleep in sludge

Or is it 'The Glorious Dead?'
They got it cos orders was cruel:
Came out cos it was 'duty',
Else face the fire squad's bitter rule.

'Eroes? D'you include the shell-shocked lad?
Nah - you fix him 'Coward' by your score!
Yet he's the one that ''ero' can address -
He stood that line 'til he could take no more

'Gallant warriors? Glorious! Ha - you mock
Each wave of blokes that filed past there t'day!
To sons role models you would 'ave us be -
Well tell 'em - take our word an' stay away!

S J Robinson

Forward Press Information

We hope you have enjoyed reading this book - and that you will continue to enjoy it in the coming years.

If you like reading and writing poetry drop us a line, or give us a call, and we'll send you a free information pack.

Alternatively if you would like to order further copies of this book or any of our other titles, then please give us a call or log onto our website at www.forwardpress.co.uk

Forward Press Information
Remus House
Coltsfoot Drive
Peterborough
PE2 9JX
(01733) 890099